PATRICIA YEO

COOKING

FROM

PATRICIA YEO

COOKING

FROM

A to Z

Patricia Yeo

AND JULIA MOSKIN

FOREWORD BY BOBBY FLAY

ST. MARTIN'S PRESS ❧ NEW YORK

PATRICIA YEO: COOKING FROM A TO Z. Copyright © 2002 by Patricia Yeo and Julia Moskin. Foreword copyright © 2002 by Bobby Flay. All rights reserved. Printed in China. No part of this book may be used or reproduced in any manner whatsoever without written permission except in the case of brief quotations embodied in critical articles or reviews. For information, address St. Martin's Press, 175 Fifth Avenue, New York, N.Y. 10010.

www.stmartins.com

Design by Kathryn Parise

All photographs by Alexander Martinez and Jody H. Fausett

ISBN 0-312-29023-3

First Edition: November 2002

10 9 8 7 6 5 4 3 2 1

To Jimmy Haber, thank you for believing in me and giving me the opportunity to be a part of AZ. Thank you for your continued support and trust. I look forward to a fruitful partnership and a long friendship.

To Michael Aviles, whose faith, love, and constant yet gentle pressure over the years have pushed me to limits I would never have dared to attempt to reach otherwise. Thank you for the love and encouragement.

CONTENTS

ACKNOWLEDGMENTS

Running a three-floor restaurant while writing this cookbook has been an inspiring experience. I owe a debt of gratitude to many wonderful people who have helped keep me sane as I grappled with this project.

To Pino Maffeo, my dear friend and chef de cuisine. Thank you for your fair-minded and patient help in guiding me through both the minor and major problems of the day, and for all your endless energy in helping make AZ what it is today. I look forward to our future endeavors together. Thank you also for the time and effort on the photographs.

To my wonderful staff at AZ, past and present, for your hard work and devotion in keeping the restaurant running seamlessly. To Michelle Vido, Claudia Crociani, and Phet Schwader for testing recipes scribbled on scraps of paper.

To Julia Moskin, who has made the experience of writing a book a lot of fun and surprisingly simple.

To Bobby Flay, who did not hesitate to agree to write the foreword for this book despite his busy life. Thank you for allowing me into a professional kitchen with no culinary experience, then making it so much fun that I never left. To Stacey Glick at Jane Dystel Literary Management for encouragement and the perfect title. To Marian Lizzi at St. Martin's Press, a wonderful and wonderfully patient editor. Thank you for your close attention and for all you've done to make this a great book.

To David Gingrass, who taught me to look at a restaurant as a whole, not just from the kitchen's perspective. To Julie Sheppard, thank you for listening to me and for our friendship. To Nicole Plue, you may have gotten away with this one, but I am enlisting your help for the next book. To Alex Martinez, who not only is responsible for the beautiful photographs in this book but also doubles as one of our waiters. To Mimi Riviera, thank you for making my calls, faxing my letters, and for doing all the little things that make my life so much easier.

And in loving memory of Barbara Tropp, who reintroduced me to Chinese cooking and inspired me in more ways than she realized.

I would also like to thank my mother, my fourth-auntie, and my sister for their love and encouragement.

FOREWORD

Way back in 1988, I was getting ready to open Miracle Grill in Manhattan's funky East Village neighborhood. I was all fired up for my experiment with the big, bold world of southwestern flavors. My culinary idols were larger-than-life Texas chefs Robert Del Grande, Dean Fearing, and Stephan Pyles, and back then there were very few women in restaurant kitchens. I would never have believed that my most trusted—and feared—assistant would turn out to be a tiny, soft-spoken female scientist with glasses, an English accent, and perfect manners (who was from Malaysia, to boot).

The first words that Patricia Yeo ever said to me were: "I have no experience. I just graduated from the New York Restaurant School last week. And I'm really a biochemist." She had never been in a working restaurant kitchen, knew nothing about the New York scene, had never heard of chipotle chile peppers, and had no idea who I was. But I could tell that she was one of the smartest people I'd ever have the chance to work with.

The entire kitchen at Miracle Grill was only big enough for two cooks besides me, so I didn't have a lot of room for error in my staff. Looking for advice, I called my dad, who said, "She sounds perfect. If she's got smarts and enthusiasm, you can teach her anything." And he was absolutely right. Patricia came in at eight in the morning and never left before midnight. She did her work, my work, and all the work that anyone else didn't get done. It was like having two of me in the restaurant—except that everyone was much more afraid of Patricia. There were plenty of cooks back then who had never worked with a woman before. But even the toughest guys quickly learned to respect her authority—or else. The most-heard word in the kitchen was "*rapido*," which Patricia expressed with a stamp of her foot and a glare through her glasses. And everybody hustled.

But that's Patricia the Enforcer. Let's talk about Patricia the Chef. First of all, she has a great palate. Initially I thought I'd have to teach her to appreciate my food, but it turned out that her Chinese background and growing up in Southeast Asia had already taught her plenty about flavor. She liked big tastes such as lime and lemon juices, fresh chiles, roasted cumin, fresh cilantro, sweet potatoes, smoked duck, pineapple and mangoes, and other ingredients that show up in both Asian and my new American cooking. Balancing lots of flavors and textures in one dish—sweet, spicy, smoky, crisp, creamy, citric, earthy—is my favorite way to cook, and I like to think that Patricia does a lot of that, too, although now with a different arsenal of ingredients. Where I'd use lime juice for tanginess, she uses Indian tamarind paste. She slices scallions; I chop chives. I stir in chipotle puree to fire up my food; she adds a teaspoon of Thai curry paste for the same effect.

Those flavors come through loud and clear in the food at Restaurant AZ and also in the recipes in the book you're holding now. Patricia may look small and dainty, but her flavors are big and strong.

Patricia and I left Miracle Grill together in 1991: I was opening Mesa Grill, and she was moving on to cook in San Francisco. But as it turned out, I couldn't open a restaurant without her. When I called for help, she was on a plane the next day. I called her in again when I opened Bolo, my Spanish-influenced restaurant, in 1994. With Patricia as my right hand (and chef de cuisine), both restaurants were big successes from the start, without the bumpy openings that many restaurants have to ride out.

The next time Patricia came back to New York, it was as the executive chef of AZ. To this day she often calls me for advice—and almost never takes it. Which is cool; she's a chef in her own right, and she knows what she likes. Here's a good example: When I tasted the first menu she developed for AZ, I told her I didn't think she should serve the duck schnitzel. "But it's good," she protested. I said, "Yes, it's great, but it's not Asian." She stuck to her guns: "So?" And a few weeks later the duck schnitzel was the first dish William Grimes of *The New York Times* mentioned in his three-star review of AZ. Apparently it's so popular that she can't take it off the menu. What more can I say? The recipe is on page 165.

—BOBBY FLAY
NEW YORK CITY

INTRODUCTION

I cook the food I love. I learned to eat in my grandmother's Chinese kitchen and on the market streets of Kuala Lumpur, the Malaysian city where we lived. But I learned to *cook* a world away, in lively restaurants in New York City and San Francisco. So how to define my food? It's light and vibrant, not quite Asian and not quite American, occasionally Indian and even slightly Mediterranean. Like all American cooking, it has layers of influence from all around the world, and it embraces everything I love to eat.

My very favorite dishes are based on both American and Asian classics. When I created the menu for Restaurant AZ, in my very first job as executive chef I jumped at the chance to serve my own interpretations of Asian dishes such as classic Peking duck with scallion pancakes; the aromatic curries I used to buy from Malaysian market vendors; and my grandmother's springy noodles in coconut broth spiked with chiles, tamarind, and lime. But I also found my mind wandering to the big-flavored dishes I'd grown to love after a decade in American restaurant kitchens, such as salmon cured in spices to make silky slices of gravlax; bitter endive and crunchy walnuts tossed into a favorite salad with creamy, pungent blue cheese; even crisp, spitting-hot veal Milanese. They all seemed ripe for an Asian-inspired renovation. The great success of AZ (including a gratifying three-star review from the *Times*) gave me the chance to play with these ideas, and the results are the recipes you'll find in these pages. They follow the basic outlines of American food but have the unmistakable zing and bright flavors of Asia.

Writing a cookbook has also given me a chance to explore the food I grew up eating and the food my extended family cooks at home. Some of my all-time favorite dishes—such as Indian curries, Thai stews, and Malaysian custards—don't fit on the menu at AZ. But their flavors are complex and fabulous, their textures velvety and comforting, and their aromas fill my house like nothing else. Wonderful cooking smells aren't something you look for in a restaurant kitchen—the high-tech exhaust and cooling systems are there to keep things as cool and clean as possible. But at home it's one of the things that makes cooking pleasurable. So I demanded my mom's recipes for my favorite Indian curries, collected my aunt's recipe for pineapple-coconut custard, and dug deep into my memory to re-create the ginger- and soy-scented liquid my grandmother used for steaming fish. The recipes have all been reworked to reflect both my taste and American home kitchens, the kind of kitchens I've been cooking in all my adult life.

Since I grew up in a Chinese family in a Southeast Asian city, the cooking style that some people call "Asian fusion" is truly my home cooking. Kuala Lumpur has always been a crossroads of Southeast Asia; its food is flavored with the traditions of India, China, Indonesia, Japan, Thailand, and on and on. At our house the cooking was mostly done by my grandmother, and I had lots of aunts who saw cooking as an important accomplishment and also a competitive sport! When they weren't actually cooking or eating, they were discussing the most traditional way to make scallion pancakes or how to thread mountains of meat onto bamboo skewers to prepare for a family *satay* party. They never sat me down and taught me to cook, but I must have absorbed their obsessions through my pores.

When I moved to the States to go to college, I didn't cook anything for years; I just put my head down and studied my biochemistry textbooks. After earning a master's degree I had three months to kill before my doctoral studies began at Princeton, so I enrolled in summer cooking school. It was little more than a whim; I just wanted to learn to feed myself. The course was a whiz-bang introduction to traditional French and new American food. Everything was very rich and refined and full of butter, and I found I liked cooking—even though the food didn't seem to have any connection to the well-spiced, big-flavored cooking I knew. And they certainly didn't teach the dishes I looked forward to on visits back to Malaysia: fresh egg noodles in spicy broths; slices of mango and jicama showered with peanuts, lime juice, and cilantro; juicy dumplings with savory dipping sauces.

It wasn't until I went to interview for a job with a young chef named Bobby Flay, stepped into his kitchen, and sniffed the air, which had familiar scents of toasted cumin, chopped cilantro, fresh lime juice, and ripe mangoes, that I found the connection between the two kinds of cooking I knew. That smell is my soul food, and I've spent every day of my life in a restaurant kitchen since I found it.

As you'll see in this book, I believe in layering flavors—sweet and sour, spicy and tangy, smoky and pungent. Of course, I also believe in using the best ingredients available. But I think that's where the art of the chef begins, not ends. Weaving flavors together, squeezing lime juice into a sauce that is already sweet with coconut, mixing a tangy tamarind glaze to cut the richness of salmon fillets, balancing the sweet of beets and the sour of oranges in a juicy salad to complement a meaty duck breast with a crisp hazelnut crust—*that's* what makes food truly transcendent.

Like all chefs, I see a huge part of my job as finding the best, freshest, finest raw materials for my craft. But I don't get preoccupied with the seasonality of ingredients to the point where it limits my cooking. The reason I don't cook with tomatoes in December is that the tomatoes don't have the right flavor, not that they don't happen to grow near New York City. I don't turn up my nose at good quality at any time of year, and I'll bet that's how you shop, too. But any cook worth her salt rejoices in the first asparagus of spring, the tomatoes and corn of summer, fall's squashes, and winter's hearty, fragrant stews. So I've given you signposts to those gloriously seasonal recipes that mark the cook's year, clearly indicating them for you to find and enjoy. I promise that you will not be limited by the season in cooking from this book; most of my recipes can be made all year round.

Here's another way I made this cookbook user-friendly: I call for very few ingredients that are hard to find or even "exotic" anymore. The array of spices at any American supermarket these days means that we can re-create the most complex Indian curries with a flip of the measuring spoons. Fresh herbs, fresh chiles, and coconut milk, mainstays of the Southeast Asian kitchen, are everywhere. In most of my dishes, friendly flavorings such as shallots, ginger, mustard, scallions, lime juice, pineapple, cilantro, asparagus, and mango are most important. They combine with touches of intense flavor from such easily available Asian basics as lemongrass, fish sauce, black beans, and cured sausage; the very first chapter of the book is dedicated to explaining and demystifying them. And I almost never suggest a special ingredient without offering a supermarket substitute. I want you to be able to use this book, not treat it as a travel guide to an exotic world!

In the ten years I've worked as a chef (mostly at Mesa Grill and Bolo in New

York, and San Francisco's China Moon and Hawthorne Lane), Americans have fallen hard for big flavors from around the world, from Mexico to the Mediterranean to China. As a result, "Asian flavors" aren't really different from "American flavors" anymore. As American food has become bolder, spicier, sweeter, and smokier, American palates have caught up with Asian tradition. Asian flavors have always been big, spicy-sweet, rich, and tangy, just like the food Americans have fallen in love with in the last twenty years. I employ the thousand (and more!)-year-old Asian tradition of culinary wisdom to create big-flavored, satisfying food. And a bonus of this cooking style is that instead of using butter and cream to boost flavor, I follow healthy Asian tradition by using vegetables, spices, and aromatics, adding body and flavor without fat.

Anyone who likes Thai or Indian or Chinese food is likely to enjoy this cooking style. It's not about any particular ethnic cuisine. It's about big flavors in balance. Balancing many flavors in a single dish is the essence of Asian cooking and, I believe, of all good cooking. It's what makes food satisfying and keeps people coming back for another taste, another spoonful, another meal. We all love the contrast of crunchy and creamy, cool and spicy, smoky and sweet, tart and rich. The radiant flavors of this food are easy to create and delightful to eat, and have a lightness that appeals to everyone. That was my goal both for AZ and for this book.

When you are the one who's cooking, I'd encourage you to trust your own palate more than any recipe. You're cooking for yourself, so only you know how much lime juice will really brighten up the rich, earthy flavor of that spicy peanut sauce; only you can find just the right balance of hot and sweet in a mustard-spiked apricot chutney. This doesn't mean that my recipes aren't precise, only that ingredients and palates vary; and in your kitchen, no one is a better cook than you. I hope this helps you enjoy cooking in the way that I do. Even after countless hours at work in the kitchen, I do still love to cook. I don't pretend that every aspect of cooking is fun; some things are just a chore (I personally hate peeling soybeans). But it should never be intimidating. If you like to eat and you know what you like, you can cook. And when you're ready for a little fun and adventure in the kitchen, I hope you'll reach for this book.

—PATRICIA YEO
NEW YORK CITY

PATRICIA YEO

COOKING

FROM

A

to

Z

Ingredients
and Basic Recipes

In this chapter I'll share with you the fundamentals of my kitchen, whether I'm cooking at home or in a restaurant. Most of them are ingredients that I simply buy; some are simple recipes that I make in big batches and use often. They are not the most important element of my food, and most have substitutes that are available in any supermarket, such as freshly grated lime zest instead of kaffir lime leaves.

I use these "exotic" ingredients for fun. Shopping for them is one of my favorite ways to spend a Sunday afternoon, sniffing out new food and exploring a new neighborhood in the process. But you can simply order all these ingredients from the sources listed on page 233.

INGREDIENTS

ALEPPO CHILI PEPPER
This Middle Eastern chili powder (Aleppo is in Syria) is mild and very fragrant. Aleppo chili adds a slightly smoky flavor as well as light heat. Hot paprika or Spanish smoked paprika can be used as substitutes. If substituting cayenne, use half the amount.

You can buy ground Aleppo chili at Middle Eastern markets. I buy it in small quantities because the smoky-sweet quality seems to fade quickly.

BLACK BEANS, CHINESE FERMENTED
Fermented black beans are salted soybeans that are allowed to ferment in the sun. (They are completely unrelated to American black or turtle beans.) Good ones should

have a pungent, almost olive-like smell. They are widely available at Asian markets in this country. Avoid beans that have visible salt crystals; the flavor is not as good on these oversalted beans, and they tend to be very hard and impossible to puree.

BUTTER, CLARIFIED

Called *ghee* in India, where it is widely used for culinary (and religious) purposes, clarified butter is pure butterfat. The milk solids that make butter creamy and milky (and which make up about 40 percent of the butter) are removed by slow cooking. Clarified butter can be heated to a much higher temperature than butter without burning.

It is used in French cooking as well as Indian, so ghee can be found in gourmet and Indian markets. You can make it by melting about twice the quantity of butter (for example, 8 tablespoons of butter will yield about 4 tablespoons of ghee) over very low heat without stirring. The milk solids will slowly separate and settle to the bottom. Skim off any froth that rises to the top. Pour off the golden oil into a glass container and leave the solids behind in the pan. Ghee lasts indefinitely, especially if refrigerated.

CHILES, THAI BIRD

Small dried chiles from Thailand, bird chiles are my favorites because they add a straightforward note of heat without a lot of extra flavor. Dried piquins or even hot red pepper flakes (1 teaspoon per chile) are a good substitute.

For fresh chiles I use jalapeños or serranos; serranos are hotter, so use less. I do not seed fresh chiles before mincing them to add to recipes, but if you prefer a less hot result, seed them first. Always wear gloves when handling fresh chiles.

COCONUT MILK, COCONUT CREAM

Canned coconut milk from Asia is my choice, especially the Thai brand Chao Koh.

When I want a thicker result, I call for "coconut cream" instead. (This is *not* the sweetened cream of coconut you can buy in the drinks section of the supermarket.) Like milk, coconut milk naturally separates in the container. If you don't shake the can before opening, you'll find a thick, creamy layer on top of the milk, making up about one-third of the can. Spoon it off and use it where coconut cream is called for.

CURRY PASTE, RED AND GREEN

Thai curry pastes are purees of chiles and aromatics, and are used to flavor a variety of curries and soups. Red curry pastes are based on dried chiles; green curry pastes on fresh chiles. Kaffir limes, cilantro, lemongrass, garlic, and shallots are often included. Curry pastes are available in Asian and gourmet markets; I use the Mae Ploy brand from Thailand. Use the pastes judiciously, because they tend to be really spicy; use less than the recipe calls for the first time, and then work your way up!

CURRY POWDER, JAVA

Indonesian curry powder, called java, is milder than Indian and contains additional ground turmeric, reflecting the local cooking style. I buy the Sun brand. You can substitute a mild Indian curry powder and add an extra half-teaspoon of turmeric to the recipe at the same time.

EGGPLANTS

Asian eggplants tend to be slimmer in shape than the big Italian ones. They are less spongy and have fewer seeds, and never need to be salted and drained before cooking. Asian eggplants can be pale lavender to dark purple in color. They are available at Asian markets, but if you can't find them, use Italian eggplants that have been salted and drained before cooking.

To choose the eggplants with the fewest seeds, pick male ones rather than female. It's easy to tell the difference: at the base, male eggplants have a long groove, and female ones have a dimple.

FISH SAUCE

Asian fish sauce, a thin, pale brown liquid, is used extensively in Thai and Vietnamese cooking. It has a very strong smell but provides a rounded, salty flavor. My favorite brand is Three Crab from Thailand. It is fairly easy to find in Asian markets; look for a section of Thai ingredients, because fish sauce is not used in China. There is no really good substitute, but you can try a combination of anchovy paste and lime juice.

Fish sauce is one of the most important ingredients in my kitchen; my staff teases that I put a dab of it behind each ear before I come to work!

FIVE-SPICE POWDER

This is a classic Chinese spice mixture of ground fennel seed, cinnamon, star anise, cloves, and Szechuan peppercorns. You can buy premixed five-spice at any Asian market. My own slightly untraditional mixture calls for 2 parts fennel seeds, 2 parts Szechuan peppercorns, 1 part star anise, 1 part cinnamon, and 1 part black peppercorns. All the spices are toasted and then ground in a spice mill.

GALANGAL

Galangal is a member of the ginger family and has a stronger, more peppery flavor. Fresh galangal is used to flavor soups and curries, but ginger can be used as a substitute. Like ginger, galangal roots should be clean and firm when you buy them, not soft.

GARAM MASALA

Meaning "hot spice" in India, garam masala is a mixture of the warm flavors of cumin, cinnamon, coriander, and others, depending on the cook. My basic garam masala consists of 1 part cinnamon, 2 parts coriander seed, 2 parts cumin, 1 part cardamom seed, and 2 parts black peppercorn. All the spices are toasted just before using and then ground in a spice mill.

GINGER JUICE

This is liquid essence of ginger, for when you want the flavor of ginger in your dish but not the texture. For each tablespoon of ginger juice, finely mince 1 tablespoon of peeled fresh ginger root and then mix in 1 tablespoon of water. Let it sit a minute or two, then squeeze out the juice in your hand or, for neater results, strain the juice through cheesecloth, squeezing to extract all the flavor from the ginger.

HOISIN SAUCE

This thick, tangy paste made from soybeans, chiles, garlic, and sesame seeds is a very common seasoning in Chinese cooking and quite addictive. Any Asian market will stock it.

KAFFIR LIME LEAVES

Kaffir limes themselves are too knobby and pithy to use in cooking, but the dried leaves of the tree impart their floral fragrance to many Thai dishes. You can buy the leaves fresh or frozen at Asian markets, particularly those that carry Thai products (they are not used in China). A teaspoon of finely grated lime zest is a reasonable substitute, but do not add it to the dish until just before serving; the delicate perfume disappears quickly.

LEMONGRASS

Lemongrass is an herb and not a citrus fruit, but its scent comes from the same chemical compounds found in lemon zest. It looks rather like a long, grassy pale-green scallion. The bottom should be moist and pungent-smelling, but the tips of the leaves may be dry. It's one of the signature flavors of Southeast Asian cooking. It can be very strong (in fact, lemongrass is closely related to citronella), so use only as much as the recipe calls for.

LENTILS

All the lentil recipes in this book call for Indian split red lentils *(masoor dal)*. They have a smooth, delicate texture and nutty flavor. They turn golden during cooking.

The lentils are small and dark pink to red, and are split into two round halves. They are sometimes also known in this country as red chief lentils. Indian golden lentils are a good substitute (they'll be called *toor dal* or *arhar dal* at Indian markets).

Regular brown and green lentils can be substituted without affecting the flavor, but the color of the dish will become rather murky.

MIRIN

This sweet rice wine is used in Japanese cooking. Kikoman Aji-Mirin is my favorite; it's not too cloying or as sweet

as the other mirins I have tasted. If you can't find it, use sake or dry vermouth and add a pinch of sugar to it.

MISO
Miso is the generic word for the family of naturally fermented soybean pastes used as seasonings and marinades in Japanese cooking. *Aga* miso, also known as red miso, is reddish brown in color and is salty and fairly mild. *Genmai* miso is brown miso made from brown rice. *Shiro* miso, my favorite, is a white (really pale yellow) miso. It is made with white rice and soybeans, and is relatively mild tasting and low in salt. It's also known as sweet or blond miso.

MUSHROOMS, DRIED
Dried Chinese mushrooms, known as black mushrooms, are simply dried shiitake mushrooms. They are available at any Asian market. To use them for cooking, cover with hot water and let soak for at least 30 minutes. Lift the mushrooms out of the bowl; a small amount of grit and dust will have settled at the bottom of the bowl. If you are going to use the liquid for cooking, strain it through cheesecloth first. Remove the stems of the mushrooms before slicing or cooking; they are too woody to eat.

The best substitute is not another dried mushroom but fresh shiitake mushrooms. Again, the stems must be removed before cooking. If you cannot find fresh shiitakes, use any flavorful fresh mushroom.

MUSTARD, SZECHUAN
A knobby, pickled root vegetable that looks like ginger but tastes like cabbage. Szechuan mustard is preserved with chile, so minced Korean kim chee or Chinese pickled mustard greens are good substitutes. Even American sauerkraut would work. Use about 1/4 cup for each knob of mustard called for.

PLUM WINE
Plum wines from Japan and China vary greatly in quality and sweetness. Japanese Gekkeikan is the brand I use. It is a wine actually made from plums, unlike the cheaper varieties that sometimes are rice wine infused with plums. Ruby port is a good substitute.

RICE

Rice is a grain, the fruit of a grass plant, and the staple food of more than half the world's population. There are hundreds of varieties of rice. To simplify the categories, I'll break them into long- and short-grain rices. Long-grain rices include jasmine, basmati, Chinese, and American Carolina. They are aromatic and tend to separate when cooked. They can all be cooked according to the method for Basic Rice (page 10). Short-grain rices include sushi, arborio, carnaroli, Camargue rice, and red rice. They also include sticky rice, sometimes called sweet or glutinous rice. Each of these rices has a slightly different cooking method. See the recipes for Basic Rice and Sticky Rice (both on page 10).

RICE NOODLES/RICE STICKS/RICE VERMICELLI

These very thin noodles are widely used in Southeast Asian cooking; you may have encountered them in the Vietnamese dishes called *bun*. Unlike Italian or Chinese wheat noodles, rice noodles do not have to be cooked but can be rehydrated in very hot water. Put the noodles in a large pot of boiling water, turn off the heat, and let soak for 5 minutes, stirring to separate the noodles, then drain. Rinse under cold running water. If not using immediately, toss the noodles in a few teaspoons of canola oil to keep them from clumping together. I buy the Erawan brand from Thailand; it is available at Asian markets.

RICE PAPER

These are the thin white sheets used in Vietnamese cooking to wrap summer rolls. They are available dried at Asian markets. I use the 8-inch rounds.

To rehydrate, season a shallow bowl of warm water with a pinch of sugar, a splash of rice vinegar, and a splash of beer. Stir to dissolve the sugar. Place one round in the water, let soak a few seconds, then lift out, shaking off excess water. Place on a lint-free kitchen towel to absorb the remaining liquid. Repeat, stacking the sheets between layers of towels. When ready to use, begin with the sheets at the bottom of the stack.

RICE WINE

Rice wines are made all over Asia. I much prefer the ones made in Japan (called *sake*) and Taiwan over the Chinese brands; they are more consistent in flavor and quality. My favorite brand of sake is Gekkeikan. Dry vermouth and bone-dry fino sherry make good substitutes.

SAMBAL

Sambal is the generic Southeast Asian term for a variety of chile-based pastes and condiments. I use the simplest, *sambal oelek*, made of just chiles, vinegar, and a little garlic. Like Tabasco, sambal can be added to a variety of dishes to provide a bit of heat; it does not require cooking.

My favorite sambal is made by Huy Fong Foods. It comes in a plastic jar with a green lid and a picture of a rooster on the label.

SAUSAGE, CHINESE

These air-dried sausages made with pork and spices are dark red and very firm. Chinese sausage is very much like salami and can be eaten raw, but it tastes best when stir-fried or steamed to render some of the fat.

The most consistent brand that I have found is Golden Mountain, manufactured in Vancouver, Canada. If necessary, a hard Italian salami can be used instead.

SHRIMP, DRIED

A popular seasoning in Asian cooking, dried shrimp have a strong smell, but their flavor is only subtly fishy, especially after cooking. I like the crunch they add to certain classic Thai dishes. Dried shrimp tend to be very salty; soak them for at least 15 minutes before using to soften them and remove some of the salt. Drain well.

Asian markets that carry Thai ingredients will have dried shrimp. The larger shrimp are more expensive, but since I usually chop them up, the size may not matter.

SUGAR, PALM

Palm sugar, made either from palm syrup or sugar cane juice, is a sweetener used in Southeast Asia, where it is known as *gula malaka* or *gula java*. Indian *jaggery*, an unrefined cane sugar, is the same thing. It comes in a solid one-pound log. Or mix dark brown sugar with a little molasses.

SZECHUAN PEPPERCORNS

Szechuan peppercorns are not really members of the pepper family (they are unrelated to black, white, green, and pink peppers); instead, they are a small berry from the prickly ash tree. These small berries are too strong to be used on their own; see recipe for Szechuan pepper salt (page 13).

TAMARIND PASTE

Tamarind paste adds a key tart note to many Indian and Southeast Asian dishes. Pure tamarind pulp comes in 8-ounce compressed blocks, available at Asian, Indian, and Middle Eastern markets. Before using, you have to soften it and remove the seeds: Place the block in a saucepan and barely cover with water. Heat to a simmer and cook, stirring, until softened, about 10 minutes. Then push the mixture through a strainer to remove the stringy bits and seeds. The paste will last indefinitely in the refrigerator.

YOGURT, THICK

I like yogurt to be thicker and creamier (more like Indian or Mediterranean yogurt) than the commercial American product. I buy Greek or Middle Eastern yogurt when I can, or goat-milk yogurt, or the dairy product called quark that is often available at health food stores.

To thicken supermarket yogurt, start with whole-milk yogurt (fat-free yogurt will not work). For 1 cup of thick yogurt, start with 2 cups of regular yogurt and pour into a strainer lined with cheesecloth or a coffee filter. Set over a bowl and refrigerate for 2 hours or so. Discard the liquid.

ZA'ATAR

A spice mix common all over the Eastern Mediterranean area, za'atar is a combination of thyme, sumac, and sesame seeds. The recipe and proportions vary according to the country (for example, Syrian za'atar includes mint), but the mix is commonly sprinkled over salads and stews, or mixed with oil to make a spread for bread. You can buy it at any Middle Eastern market.

INGREDIENTS

BASIC RICE

Depending on what you're serving, you'll need about 1/3 cup of raw rice per person. One cup of raw rice will yield about 3 cups of cooked.

Pour the rice into a heavy saucepan. Pour in water to cover the rice by about three-fourths of an inch. To test it, let the rice settle, then rest your fingertip on top of the rice. The water should come up to the first joint of your finger. Do not add salt. Bring the rice and water to a boil over high heat. Stir well, reduce the heat to as low as possible, and cover tightly. Let cook, undisturbed, for 20 minutes. Turn off the heat and let rest, undisturbed, 10 minutes more. You can set aside the rice at this point; depending on the temperature of your kitchen and the weight of the pot, it will stay hot for up to 1 hour. When ready to serve, fluff with a pair of chopsticks.

STICKY RICE

Depending on what you're serving, you'll need about 1/3 cup of raw rice per person. One cup of raw rice will yield about 3 cups of cooked.

Pour the rice into a saucepan. For each cup of rice, pour in 1 1/4 cups of water. Do not add salt. Bring the rice and water to a boil over high heat. Stir well, reduce the heat to as low as possible, and cover tightly. Let cook, undisturbed, for 20 minutes. Turn off the heat and let rest, undisturbed, 10 minutes more. You can set aside the rice at this point; depending on the temperature of your kitchen and the weight of the pot, it will stay hot for up to 1 hour.

ROASTED PEPPERS

For the best results when roasting bell peppers and chiles, such as poblanos, simply stick the pepper on a long-handled fork and hold it over the open flame of your gas burner. Turn it frequently until the skin is completely charred, then wrap in a brown paper bag and allow to steam for 5 minutes or until cool enough to handle (this helps the skins come away from the flesh). Use your hands to peel and seed the peppers. Refrain from rinsing the roasted pepper, because the water will wash away all the lovely roasted and charred flavors.

Some people roast their peppers in a very hot oven. This isn't my favorite method because by the time the skin chars and blisters, the flesh of the pepper is overcooked and slimy. But if you have a large quantity of peppers to roast and not enough time, rub the peppers with oil before placing them on a cookie sheet in a 500-degree oven. Roast about 15 minutes, until softened and blistered, then steam, peel, and seed as above.

TOASTED NUTS AND COCONUT

Nuts are toasted to deepen their flavors. Preheat the oven to 350 degrees and spread the nuts on a sheet pan. Toast for 6 to 10 minutes, stirring often after the first 5 minutes, until the nuts are fragrant and slightly browned. Check them often since they can burn quickly. Small amounts can be toasted in a toaster oven.

TOASTED SPICES AND SEEDS

I almost always toast whole spices before grinding them, to release their freshest flavors. (Preground spices cannot be toasted; they will burn.)

Heat a heavy skillet and add the spices (don't use any oil). Shake the pan and stir the spices often. As soon as the spices are darkened and fragrant, remove them from the hot pan immediately or they will keep cooking and burn. Let cool, then grind in a coffee grinder. I keep separate grinders for spices, because I don't want my coffee to taste of spices, and vice versa!

SCALLION OIL

MAKES
1 CUP

This versatile oil can be used just like canola oil. It's flavored with scallions, but since it contains no solids, it won't spoil. You can even use it as a cooking oil because it won't burn. I like it best in salads or tossed with rice noodles.

4 fat scallions, white parts smashed and
   green parts roughly cut up
5 peppercorns

1 bay leaf
1 cup canola oil

Combine all the ingredients in a small saucepan and heat over high heat just until the oil boils. Turn off the heat and let steep for 10 minutes. Strain into an airtight container. Will keep indefinitely.

Szechuan Pepper Salt

This is a classic Chinese seasoning. Szechuan peppercorns taste too strong to be used on their own, and they contain a small black seed that must be removed before cooking. The creative solution is this pungent pale gray mixture.

1 cup kosher salt

1 cup Szechuan peppercorns

Combine the salt and peppercorns in a large skillet over high heat and cook, stirring often, until the salt starts to turn gray, about 30 minutes. Immediately remove from the skillet and set aside to cool. Grind the mixture in a powerful blender or a spice or coffee grinder. The peppercorns have a hard black seed at the center that will not grind; sift the mixture through a flour sifter or sieve to remove the seeds. Use immediately or transfer to a glass jar and cover tightly. Will keep indefinitely.

Chicken Stock

This is the easiest, most basic, and most useful stock. In a pinch it can almost always be used instead of Shellfish Stock or Beef Stock (these recipes follow). When I call for lightly salted chicken stock, this is what I use.

In many recipes there's nothing wrong with using low-salt canned stock. My food is highly seasoned, and any "canned" flavor usually disappears. Buy canned stocks with the fewest number of additives and the smallest amount of salt. The glazes and stock bases available at many gourmet stores can be very good, but many are over-salted or too sweet. Taste any stock before using it; if it doesn't taste pretty good on its own, it won't taste good in the dish.

4 pounds chicken bones (preferably necks and backs) or chicken wings, skin and excess fat removed

3 medium carrots, peeled and coarsely chopped

2 cups coarsely chopped onions

1 cup coarsely chopped celery

2 bay leaves

2 tablespoons black peppercorns

1 small bunch fresh thyme or 2 teaspoons dried

Rinse the bones well to remove any blood. Place in a stockpot. Add about 3 quarts water, until the bones are well covered. Bring to a boil over high heat, then lower to a bare simmer. Simmer, uncovered, for 2 hours, skimming fat and scum off the top frequently. Add the remaining ingredients and simmer 1 hour more.

Strain through a fine sieve to remove all the solids. Let cool and refrigerate until ready to use, up to 3 days, or freeze indefinitely.

Beef Stock

8 pounds veal bones (you can buy these from your butcher)

2 teaspoons canola oil

3 medium carrots, peeled and coarsely chopped

2 cups coarsely chopped onions

1 cup coarsely chopped celery

2 cups red wine

½ cup ruby port

1 cup chopped fresh or canned tomatoes or ¼ cup tomato paste mixed with 1 cup water

3 tablespoons black peppercorns

2 bay leaves

1 small bunch fresh thyme or 2 teaspoons dried

Heat the oven to 400 degrees. Rub the bones with the oil, place in a roasting pan, and roast for 90 minutes. Add the carrots, onions, and celery to the pan and continue roasting 30 minutes more.

Transfer the bones and vegetables to a stockpot and place the hot roasting pan on top of the stove. Pour the wine and port into the roasting pan and stir, scraping to remove all the browned bits from the bottom and sides of the pan. Pour into the stockpot. Add 4 quarts of water. Bring to a boil over high heat, then reduce to a bare simmer. Simmer, uncovered, for 1 hour, skimming fat and scum off the top frequently. Add the remaining ingredients and simmer 5 hours more.

Strain through a fine sieve to remove all the solids. Let cool and refrigerate until ready to use, up to 3 days, or freeze indefinitely.

SHELLFISH STOCK

MAKES
ABOUT
2 1/2 QUARTS

3 pounds whole shrimp or lobster
   carcasses, tail and claw meat removed
4 tablespoons canola oil
3 medium carrots, peeled and coarsely
   chopped
2 cups coarsely chopped onions
1 cup coarsely chopped celery
1 head garlic (remove excess skin from
   the outside but do not peel), cut in
   half crosswise

1 cup brandy
1 cup chopped fresh or canned tomatoes
   or 1/4 cup tomato paste mixed with 1
   cup water
2 tablespoons black peppercorns
2 bay leaves
1 small bunch basil

Heat the oven to 400 degrees. Rub the shrimp or lobster carcasses with 2 tablespoons oil, place in a roasting pan, and roast for 25 minutes. Transfer to a stockpot. Add the remaining 2 tablespoons oil, carrots, onions, celery, and garlic. Cook over medium heat for 10 minutes, stirring occasionally. Turn off the heat and add the brandy. Turn the heat to high and simmer for 5 minutes, then add the tomatoes, peppercorns, and bay leaves. Add 2 1/2 quarts of water. Bring to a boil over high heat, then reduce to a bare simmer. Simmer, uncovered, for 30 minutes, skimming fat and scum off the top frequently. Add the basil and continue cooking 30 minutes more.

Strain through a fine sieve to remove all the solids. Let cool and refrigerate until ready to use, up to 3 days, or freeze indefinitely.

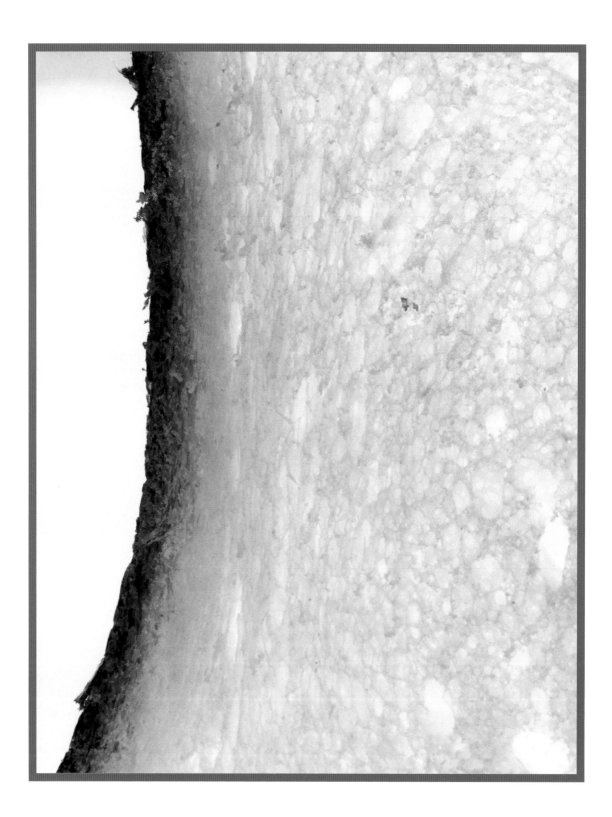

Chutneys and Flatbreads

APRICOT MUSTARD CHUTNEY

CORN AND PEPPER RELISH WITH BASIL, MINT, AND CILANTRO

CRUNCHY CUCUMBER-YOGURT-CUMIN DIP (*RAITA*)

CILANTRO CHUTNEY WITH COCONUT

CURRIED LENTIL PUREE

GINGERED CHICKPEA CHUTNEY

SWEET-AND-SOUR EGGPLANT (*CAPONATA*)

ONION CUMIN JAM

DRIED CRANBERRY AND KUMQUAT CHUTNEY

ZA'ATAR CRISPS

WHOLE WHEAT *CHAPPATI* BREADS

Apricot Mustard Chutney

MAKES
4 CUPS

Every meal at Restaurant AZ begins with a bang: a plate of crisp flatbread and three lively chutneys instead of butter. Chutneys are traditionally served with a meal, but I think they make wonderful appetizers beforehand. I offer one spicy, one sweet, and one herbal chutney each day to impress my guests with a sense of the exciting tastes to come—but I sometimes feel like a bit of a trickster. That's because chutneys are so easy to put together, and the ingredients create their own flavor complexity.

This is one of my sweet chutney mainstays, with additional hot notes that everyone—particularly those who like honey mustard—seems to love. It includes mustard in no less than five different forms. It's wonderful as a dip, with grilled chicken, or on a sandwich.

1 teaspoon canola oil
½ cup sliced shallots
2 tablespoons minced fresh ginger
½ teaspoon hot red pepper flakes
2 tablespoons yellow mustard seeds
2 tablespoons black mustard seeds
2 cups dried apricots (if very dry and
  leathery, soak in warm water for 1 hour)

1 cup lightly salted Chicken Stock (page
  13), vegetable stock, or water
1 cup orange juice
½ cup champagne or white wine vinegar
2 tablespoons dry mustard powder
½ cup Dijon mustard
½ cup coarse-grain mustard

Heat the oil in a medium-size heavy pot over medium-high heat. Add the shallots and cook, stirring often, until softened and lightly browned, about 10 minutes. Add the ginger, pepper flakes, and both kinds of mustard seeds and cook, stirring, until the seeds start to pop and the black ones turn gray, about 3 minutes.

Add the apricots, stock, juice, and vinegar and lower the heat to a simmer. Simmer until the apricots are very soft, about 1 hour. Let cool slightly, then puree in a food processor (or use a hand blender) until almost smooth. Mix the mustard powder with 2 tablespoons water to make a smooth paste, then mix into the chutney. Mix in the Dijon and coarse mustards.

Serve immediately or refrigerate in an airtight container for up to 1 month. The chutney will thicken as it sits, so you may wish to thin it with water and stir well before using.

CORN AND PEPPER RELISH WITH BASIL, MINT, AND CILANTRO

SUMMER

When I'm firing up the grill for a summer dinner, I like to get all my cooking done over the coals—why waste any of that great heat? As soon as the fire is ready, I toss on ears of corn, red bell peppers, and poblano chiles to give them a quick roast, then dice them up. The classic Southeast Asian herbs of basil, cilantro, and mint add freshness, color, and zip to this quintessentially American side dish. You can serve it on grilled bread or flatbread, or as a relish with any grilled fish, chicken, or meat.

If grilling is not part of your dinner plan, you can rework the recipe by roasting the peppers on the stove as described on page 10 and tossing the corn kernels in a little oil in a very hot skillet.

6 ears of corn, husked and grilled just
   until browned, kernels cut off
   (about 3 cups kernels)
2 red bell peppers, roasted, peeled,
   seeded, and diced (page 10)
2 poblano chiles, roasted, peeled, seeded,
   and diced (page 10)
2 jalapeño chiles, minced
2 kaffir lime leaves (page 4) *or*
   2 teaspoons freshly grated lime zest

Freshly squeezed juice of 2 limes
½ cup chopped cilantro
¼ cup shredded basil
¼ cup shredded mint
2 teaspoons canola oil
1 to 2 teaspoons sugar, or to taste
Fish sauce (page 3)

Gently fold all the ingredients together. Season with sugar and fish sauce to taste. Serve within 2 hours at room temperature.

CRUNCHY CUCUMBER-YOGURT-CUMIN DIP (*RAITA*)

MAKES ABOUT 2 CUPS

Hot Indian curries are always served with a cooling raita, *plain yogurt mixed with juicy cucumber and mint leaves to quench the fire. I love* raita *so much that I couldn't resist making it more of a centerpiece than a sauce. I thicken the yogurt and fold in a variety of aromatics and crisp vegetables: cucumber, onion, and even tart apple to make it chunky and creamy. It is almost like a Waldorf salad, but much lighter and tastier. And it still makes a great side dish for my favorite curries, or a stunning dip for Za'atar Crisps (page 29).*

1 cup thick yogurt (page 9)
1 cucumber, peeled, seeded, and cut into
   1/2-inch dice
1 small red onion, minced
1 tart apple, such as Granny Smith,
   peeled, cored, and chopped
2 teaspoons cumin seeds, toasted and
   ground (page 12)

2 teaspoons garam masala (page 4)
1 teaspoon minced fresh ginger
1/2 cup chopped mint
Zest and juice of 1 lime
Kosher salt and freshly ground black
   pepper

Fold all the ingredients together and season to taste with salt and pepper. Serve immediately or refrigerate up to 8 hours. Stir well before serving and serve chilled.

CILANTRO CHUTNEY
WITH COCONUT

This green chutney is heaven for cilantro lovers like me. I cut the cilantro with parsley to make it more substantial (if you cook with cilantro, you've probably noticed that it tends to almost disappear as you chop it). Pungent garlic, tart vinegar, and rich nuts show off the herbal flavors. This chutney makes a wonderful spark for mild curries, an appetite-stimulating dip, or an addictive sauce for grilled fish or chicken.

2 cups cilantro leaves

2 cups parsley leaves

1 clove garlic

¼ cup rice wine vinegar

1 cup coconut, toasted (page 11) and cooled

¼ cup macadamia or pine nuts, toasted (page 11) and cooled

1 cup canola oil

Kosher salt and freshly ground black pepper

In a blender or food processor, puree all the ingredients together. Season with salt and pepper to taste. Serve immediately or refrigerate up to 1 day. Serve at room temperature.

Curried Lentil Puree

Lentils have a wonderful knack for picking up flavors. They can be earthy, spicy, herbal, or anything you want them to be. This is my favorite combination of spices, rooted in the Indian tradition of dals, *spiced lentil stews eaten daily with* chappati *bread (see page 30). I use less liquid than I would for a dal to make this thick, smooth puree, a perfect dip for flatbread or a side dish for lamb or any curry.*

The yogurt adds a richness and tart flavor that I love, but the puree would still be creamy and delicious without it.

2 tablespoons canola oil
1 large onion, chopped
½ cup chopped fresh ginger
¼ cup chopped garlic
½ to 2 teaspoons cayenne pepper, to taste
2 tablespoons ground cumin
2 tablespoons ground coriander

2 cups red lentils (page 5)
1 cup chopped tomatoes, fresh or canned
2 cups lightly salted Chicken Stock (page 13), vegetable stock, or water
Kosher salt and freshly ground black pepper
½ cup chopped cilantro
1 cup thick yogurt (page 9; optional)

Heat the oil in a large, heavy pot over high heat. Add the onion and cook, stirring, until it begins to brown, 8 to 10 minutes. Add the ginger and garlic, reduce the heat, and continue cooking until the onion is lightly browned, about 10 minutes more.

Add the cayenne, cumin, and coriander, and cook, stirring, for 1 minute. Add the lentils, tomatoes, and stock, and bring to a boil. Cover, lower the heat, and simmer gently, stirring often to prevent the lentils from sticking to the bottom. Cook until the lentils are very tender and the liquid has been absorbed, 20 to 30 minutes. Puree with a hand blender (or mix vigorously with a sturdy whisk to break up the lentils) until thick and creamy. Season to taste with salt and pepper. If serving hot, fold in the cilantro and yogurt, and serve immediately. *(The recipe can be made in advance up to this point and kept refrigerated up to 2 days.)*

Just before serving, fold in the cilantro and yogurt. Serve at room temperature.

GINGERED CHICKPEA CHUTNEY

MAKES
4 CUPS

If you think chickpeas are bland, you haven't tasted them cooked the Indian way. Chickpeas simmered in a bright gingery tomato sauce make a delicious staple all over India. This chutney takes that dish and simmers it all the way down to a moist, fragrantly spiced puree that really sparks appetites. It is like the best version of hummus you can imagine.

Use the chutney as a dip or as a side dish for roast lamb or chicken. Or blend the mixture with a quart of stock to make a wonderful, smooth, rich-tasting soup.

1 ½ cups dried chickpeas *or* 4 cups
   drained canned chickpeas
½ cup canola oil
1 large onion, chopped
¼ cup minced fresh ginger
2 tablespoons garam masala
   (page 4)
½ cup chopped tomatoes,
   fresh or canned

¼ cup white wine
½ teaspoon Aleppo pepper (page 1) or
   paprika or cayenne to taste
Freshly squeezed juice of 1 lemon
Kosher salt
½ cup chopped cilantro

If using dried chickpeas, soak them overnight in plenty of cold unsalted water. When ready to cook, drain the chickpeas and add plenty of fresh water to the pot. Bring to a boil, lower the heat, and simmer gently until tender, 1 ½ to 3 hours depending on the age and size of the chickpeas. Do not salt the water because salt can toughen the skins of the chickpeas. Drain and set aside in a bowl.

If using canned chickpeas, drain well and place in a serving bowl.

In a large skillet, heat 2 tablespoons oil over high heat. Add the onion, ginger, and garam masala, and cook, stirring occasionally, until the onion is soft. Add the tomatoes and white wine, and simmer, stirring often, until the mixture is almost dry.

Add the onion mixture to the chickpeas and mix well with a sturdy spoon (or use a potato masher), breaking up some of the chickpeas to create a chunky puree.

Let cool to room temperature. Add the Aleppo pepper, lemon juice, and remaining oil, and mix well. Season to taste with salt.

(The recipe can be made in advance up to this point and kept refrigerated up to 2 days. Bring to room temperature before serving.)

Just before serving, stir in the cilantro and add salt and lemon juice to taste.

Sweet-and-Sour Eggplant (Caponata)

Caponata, *from the southern Italian island of Sicily, is one of my favorite dishes in the world. Like many Thai dishes, it seems to hit every taste bud with its salty, sweet, tangy, earthy, fruity, and rich ingredients. A traditional* caponata *is slowly cooked into a chunky, delicious sort of sludge with savory shreds of capers, olives, and raisins. But I like to play up the contrasts in the recipe by combining the soft eggplants and red peppers with crisp celery and onion and crunchy pine nuts as well.*

1 tablespoon canola oil
5 Asian eggplants (page 3), peeled and
    cut into ¼-inch cubes
2 cloves garlic, chopped
½ cup chopped onion
½ cup chopped celery
1 large red pepper, roasted, peeled,
    seeded, and diced (page 10)
¼ cup capers, drained

½ cup chopped green olives
¼ cup pine nuts, toasted (page 11)
½ cup golden raisins
½ cup red wine vinegar
½ cup olive oil
Kosher salt and freshly ground black
    pepper
½ cup chopped cilantro or parsley

Heat half of the oil in a nonstick pan over high heat. Add half of the eggplants and garlic, and cook, stirring, until the eggplants are tender and lightly browned. Transfer to a mixing bowl. Repeat with the remaining oil, eggplants, and garlic.

Meanwhile, bring a pot of water to a boil. Add the onion and celery, and boil until just tender, about 3 minutes. Drain well and add to the eggplants. Add the remaining ingredients (except the cilantro) and mix well. Season to taste with salt and pepper.

(The recipe can be made in advance up to this point and kept refrigerated up to 1 week.) Just before serving, taste for salt and pepper, and stir in the cilantro. Serve at room temperature.

Onion Cumin Jam

This intense sweet-tart jam (which happens to be extremely low in fat) is packed with the golden caramel flavor of slow-cooked onions. It's very easy to make. You do have to be patient about browning the onions, but you can do other things in the kitchen as they cook. Just give the mixture a stir every time you walk by the pot—that's the rule in my kitchen!

The slow cooking evaporates all the water in the onions, concentrating the flavor. Then you simply spike the mixture with earthy cumin and tangy sherry vinegar. And that's all there is to it! Serve the jam with Za'atar Crisps (page 29) or with roast chicken or lamb.

2 teaspoons canola oil
5 onions, chopped
1/3 cup coarsely chopped garlic
2 tablespoons cumin seeds, toasted and
   ground (page 12)

1/3 cup aged sherry vinegar
Kosher salt and freshly ground black
   pepper

Heat the oil in a nonstick pan over medium-high heat. Add the onions and garlic, lower the heat, and cook gently, stirring often, until the onions are very tender but not browned, about 20 minutes. Then raise the heat to high and cook, stirring often, until the onions are well browned and caramelized, about 10 minutes more. Transfer to a blender or food processor with the cumin and vinegar. Puree just until smooth and season to taste with salt and pepper.

Dried Cranberry and Kumquat Chutney

FALL / WINTER

There's no livelier flavor combination than cranberry and orange: Both fruits are bracingly tart, sweet, and juicy. Kumquats are substituted for the oranges in this complex winter fruit chutney, which always adorns my Thanksgiving table.

The entire kumquat is edible, so you can include the peel as well as the juicy flesh without worrying about the bitter pith in between. The shallots and brown sugar make this wonderful with poultry and meat, and I also use it as the base for a lively vinaigrette: Just whisk in canola oil and extra vinegar to taste.

2 cups dried cranberries
1 cup thinly sliced shallots
1 cup halved kumquats, pits removed with
   the tip of a sharp knife

1 cup white wine vinegar
1 cup light brown sugar
Kosher salt and freshly ground black
   pepper

Combine all the ingredients except the salt and pepper in a pot and bring to a simmer. Simmer until most of the liquid has evaporated and the cranberries are juicy and tender, approximately 10 to 15 minutes. Add water as needed if the mixture starts to dry out. Season to taste with salt and pepper. *(The recipe can be made and kept refrigerated up to 1 week.)* Serve at room temperature.

Za'atar Crisps

Since we opened Restaurant AZ, we must have made a million loaves of this crunchy, fragrant, liberally spiced flatbread. It is the very first thing you taste when you dine with us, accompanied by chutneys, curries, or spreads for dipping. The spices are strong and pungent without being overwhelming, and they embrace the Asian, Indian, and Mediterranean flavors of my food. The crisps are also wonderful on their own or when broken into pieces and tossed into salads.

Sumac is a strong Middle Eastern spice; I love its lemony flavor. If you can't find it, the crisps will still be excellent.

5 pita breads
1 tablespoon za'atar (page 9)
1 tablespoon Szechuan pepper salt
  (page 13)

1 tablespoon sumac (optional; see note
  above)
¼ cup melted butter

Heat the oven to 300 degrees.

Using the tip of a sharp knife, cut around the circumference of the pita breads and gently separate the two sides. Arrange the 10 thin pita rounds on two sheet pans.

Mix the za'atar, Szechuan pepper salt, and sumac together. Brush the rough (interior) sides of each pita round with melted butter, then sprinkle with the spice mix. Bake for 5 minutes, then turn off the heat and leave in the oven for another 15 minutes. Break the rounds into large pieces for serving. *(The recipe can be made and stored in an airtight container up to 3 days.)*

WHOLE WHEAT
CHAPPATI BREADS

This is the daily bread of India: a soft, nutty flatbread cooked on a griddle until blistered and toasty. Chappatis (also called rotis) are perfect for dipping into liberally spiced curries, chutneys, and soups. Whole wheat flour is very finely ground in India; called atta, you can find it readily at Indian grocery stores. But a combination of whole wheat and all-purpose flour works well, too.

I brush each chappati with melted butter (sometimes infused with peppercorns or other spices) as it comes off the griddle.

1 ½ cups whole wheat flour
½ cup all-purpose flour

½ cup warm water
Melted butter for brushing (optional)

Sift the flours together into the bowl of a mixer fitted with a dough hook or a food processor fitted with a plastic blade. Add the water, 1 tablespoon at a time, mixing or pulsing after each addition. Knead or process until the dough is soft and elastic, about 10 minutes. Turn the dough out onto a work surface and knead a few more times by hand.

Form the dough into a log and cut the log into 12 equal pieces. Roll out each piece with a rolling pin into a circle 7 to 8 inches in diameter. Make a stack of the dough circles and keep them covered with a slightly damp cloth.

Heat a cast-iron skillet or griddle or a heavy nonstick skillet over high heat until a drop of water sizzles and evaporates immediately when dropped into the pan. Add 1 *chappati* and let it cook until the bottom is speckled with dark brown, about 1 minute. Turn and cook the second side about 30 seconds, pressing down on the chappati with the back of a spatula as it puffs up. Transfer to a plate, brush lightly with melted butter (if using), and cover with a cloth to keep warm. Repeat with the remaining dough. Serve warm.

(The recipe can be made in advance up to this point and frozen or refrigerated up to 1 week.) Rewarm in the oven or in a skillet before serving.

Cold and Hot Appetizers

YELLOWTAIL TARTARE WITH SCALLION OIL
AND LEMON ZEST

SPICY TUNA TARTARE WITH CUCUMBER AND
GREEN APPLE

SASHIMI WITH SIZZLING GARLIC AND LIME
SAUCE

LEMONGRASS GRAVLAX WITH RICE BLINI

COLD SPICY SESAME NOODLES WITH CRISP
VEGETABLES

INDIAN VEGETABLE FRITTERS WITH
CILANTRO-YOGURT PESTO

POTATO SPRINGROLL KNISHES WITH
CRÈME FRAÎCHE AND CAVIAR

GINGER-LACQUERED HOT CHICKEN WINGS

EASY DUCK FOIE GRAS MOUSSE

BARBECUED SHORT RIBS WITH GREEN
PEPPERCORN–APPLE GLAZE

CURRIED LAMB *SAMOSAS* WITH GRILLED
PEACH-MINT *RAITA*

Yellowtail Tartare with Scallion Oil and Lemon Zest

This simple starter is easy to make and magically flavorful; yellowtail and scallion have a natural affinity for each other. Aromatic lemon zest brings out the best of both. You can serve this tartare on cucumber slices or endive spears, and I happen to know that it's extremely delicious scooped onto potato chips! These days you can find fancy potato and other vegetable chips, such as Terra Chips, in supermarkets.

I like to serve two or more tartares together as an appetizer. This one and the one that follows make an excellent pair, two variations on a single theme.

10 to 12 ounces sushi-quality yellowtail
 (*hamachi*), tuna, or sea bass, cut into
 ½-inch dice
2 tablespoons Scallion Oil (page 12)
2 tablespoons minced scallion, light green
 parts only

Freshly grated zest of 1 lemon
Kosher salt and freshly ground black
 pepper

Just before serving, toss the fish in the oil until each piece is lightly coated. Add the remaining ingredients and fold together. Add salt and pepper to taste. Serve immediately.

SPICY TUNA TARTARE WITH CUCUMBER AND GREEN APPLE

Tuna tartare, a close cousin to sushi, has become incredibly popular in the last few years. And why not? Silky little cubes of fine fish, lightly tossed with bright seasonings, make a wonderful appetizer. My favorite sushi is the kind with spicy mayonnaise, so I decided to include that in my tartare. It couldn't be easier to make. The rich, aromatic tartare needs crunch to set it off, so I spoon it onto tangy slices of green apple and top it all off with whole black sesame seeds.

"Sushi-grade" means that the fish is both very high in quality and very fresh. When making tartares, chefs always toss the fish with oil before adding any other ingredients, to create a protective coating for the fish and to make it shine.

4 teaspoons mayonnaise
½ teaspoon *sambal* (page 8), or to taste
10 to 12 ounces sushi-grade tuna,
   cut into ¼-inch dice
2 teaspoons canola oil
2 teaspoons minced scallion, white part
   only
2 teaspoons freshly squeezed lemon juice

2 teaspoons dark sesame oil
Kosher salt and freshly ground black
   pepper
1 small cucumber, sliced ¼-inch thick
1 small Granny Smith apple, peeled and
   cut into ¼-inch-thick wedges
Black sesame seeds, for garnish

In a small bowl, mix the mayonnaise and *sambal* together. Add more *sambal* until the mayonnaise is as spicy as you like it.

Just before serving, place the tuna in a bowl and gently mix in the canola oil, making sure each piece is covered with a thin film of oil. Add the mayonnaise, scallion, lemon juice, and sesame oil. Mix well and season to taste with salt and pepper. Spoon the tartare in small mounds onto the cucumber rounds and apple wedges. Arrange on a serving platter and sprinkle the tartare with sesame seeds. Serve immediately.

SASHIMI WITH SIZZLING GARLIC AND LIME SAUCE

Cool, silky fish with a hot, fragrant dressing is one of my favorite food creations. It's also very elegant and shockingly simple to make. The hot oil takes the raw edge off the fish while releasing all the scent and flavor of the garlic, soy, and lime. The bits of cucumber, apples, and greens are easy additions that provide even more lively contrast.

The optional crisped rice provides a wonderful crunch; in addition to being a lovely garnish, I can attest that it makes an addictive, delicious snack on its own.

**FOR THE CRISPED RICE
(OPTIONAL):**
2 cups canola oil
1 cup cooked rice
Kosher salt and freshly ground black
    pepper

FOR THE SASHIMI:
12 ounces sushi-quality fish fillets,
    preferably fluke, yellowtail *(hamachi)*,
    or tuna
1 tablespoon soy sauce *or* 2 tablespoons
    Soy-Lime Vinaigrette (page 59)

¼ cup canola oil
1 tablespoon finely minced garlic
Freshly grated zest and freshly squeezed
    juice of 2 limes
Kosher salt and freshly ground black
    pepper
1 tart apple such as Granny Smith, peeled
    and cut into ¼-inch dice
1 small cucumber, peeled, seeded, and cut
    into ¼-inch dice
½ cup baby salad greens

Make the rice (if using): Heat the oil in a deep pot over high heat. When it ripples, add a few grains of rice. When the rice bubbles and begins to brown, the oil is hot. Add the remaining rice and stir well to break up the grains (small clumps are okay). Fry until golden brown, then strain. Season to taste with salt and pepper.

Make the sashimi: Slice the fish very, very thin and divide the slices among serving plates. *(The recipe can be made in advance up to this point and kept refrigerated up to 1 hour. Tightly wrap each plate with plastic wrap, pressing the wrap against the surface of the fish.)*

Just before serving, sprinkle the cold fish with soy sauce. Heat the oil in a small saucepan until very hot. Add the garlic and cook, swirling the pan, until just golden. Turn off the heat and whisk in the lime zest and juice. Season to taste with salt and pepper. Drizzle the hot mixture over the fish. Sprinkle each serving with apple, cucumber, baby greens, and a spoonful of crisped rice. Serve immediately.

LEMONGRASS GRAVLAX
WITH RICE BLINI

MAKES
8 TO 12
SERVINGS

Everyone loves cool, luscious gravlax, spice-cured salmon that is easy to make and absolutely delicious. My salt-and-sugar cure brings out the natural flavor of the salmon, and I use aromatics—lemon zest and lemongrass—to create a perfume that plays on the natural affinity of salmon and lemon.

I sometimes add a dollop of caviar crème fraîche, an easy (and sneaky!) mixture that stretches a little bit of caviar a long way. Simply mix 1 tablespoon of caviar or roe into ½ cup of crème fraîche. The cream takes on the flavor of the caviar.

1 piece (2 to 3 pounds) salmon fillet with the skin on

FOR THE CURING MIXTURE:
1 pound light brown sugar
1 pound kosher salt
1 cup finely chopped lemongrass (trim off the tough ends before chopping)

½ cup freshly grated lemon zest
½ cup coriander seeds, toasted (page 12) and coarsely crushed
Canola oil
Rice Blini (recipe follows; optional)
Caviar crème fraîche (recipe above, optional)
Snipped chives, for garnish

At least 2 days before serving, cure the salmon: With a fork, lightly prick the thicker parts all over (this will help it absorb the flavors completely). Mix the curing mixture ingredients together thoroughly.

In a roasting pan large enough to hold the whole fillet, spread a thin layer of the curing mixture. Place the fillet on top and pour on the remaining mixture. Pack it well over the fillet, making sure it is completely covered. Cover tightly with plastic wrap. Refrigerate for about 36 hours, or up to 48 hours.

Under cool running water, gently but thoroughly rinse off the curing mixture. Pat dry. Rub the salmon lightly all over with oil, wrap in plastic, and refrigerate until ready to serve, up to 1 week.

When ready to serve, slice the salmon very, very thin. If desired, serve with Rice Blini and caviar crème fraîche (see above). Sprinkle with the chives.

COLD
AND HOT
APPETIZERS

Rice Blini

You can complete this easy batter a day in advance, right up to the point of whipping the egg whites and adding them to the batter. That should be done right before you cook the blini. To eat, drape thin slices of gravlax on top of each blini.

1 cup basmati rice, soaked overnight in water to cover
1 cup Indian red lentils (page 5), soaked overnight in 2 cups water, or additional rice
½ cup all-purpose flour

2 teaspoons baking powder
3 whole eggs, beaten
1 tablespoon minced fresh ginger
1 tablespoon ground coriander
3 egg whites
Butter for cooking

Place the rice and lentils, along with their soaking liquids, in a blender. Puree until smooth, adding more water if needed to make a liquid about the texture of heavy cream. The liquid won't be smooth; bits of rice and lentil will be visible. Transfer to a mixing bowl and mix in the flour and baking powder. Mix in the eggs, ginger, and coriander.

Whip the egg whites until soft peaks form, then fold into the lentil-rice mixture.

Heat the oven to 200 degrees and place an ovenproof plate inside. Heat a skillet over medium-high heat. Add a pat of butter and swirl to coat the bottom of the pan as it melts. Drop the batter by tablespoons into the pan, making sure not to crowd it. Cook each blini on one side until the top bubbles and forms craters; this is the sign that it's ready to turn. Turn and cook about 1 minute more, until the center of the blini is firm, not mushy. Transfer to the warm plate and place in the oven. Repeat with the remaining batter. When all the blini are made, cover the plate with foil and keep warm until ready to serve, up to 2 hours. Serve as soon as possible.

COLD SPICY SESAME NOODLES WITH CRISP VEGETABLES

I could eat this classic every single day. Making your own dressing from freshly toasted sesame seeds, aromatic shallots, and dark-roasted sesame oil transforms the dish into a lively appetizer—or even a main course with the addition of grilled shrimp or chicken satays *(page 204). I also toss in lots of crunchy vegetables to contrast with the soft noodles. In Chinese legend, cutting the noodles could bring bad luck, so just to be safe, I leave the strands long and toss with the dressing using my hands and a large bowl. It also works better than any other method.*

FOR THE DRESSING:
¾ cup plus 1 tablespoon (4 ounces)
   sesame seeds
7 tablespoons peanut oil
3 medium or 2 large shallots, sliced
1 clove garlic, minced
1 tablespoon dark sesame oil
2 tablespoons soy sauce, or to taste
¼ cup rice wine vinegar
¼ cup sugar
1 teaspoon *sambal* (page 8)

FOR THE NOODLES:
12 to 16 ounces fresh Chinese egg
   noodles or long, thin fresh pasta
3 tablespoons peanut oil
2 tablespoons chopped cilantro
1 cup snow peas, blanched in boiling water
   and thinly sliced
1 small red bell pepper, seeded and thinly
   sliced
1 cup thinly sliced daikon radish or
   cucumber
1 cup whole cilantro leaves
½ cup chopped peanuts
1 cup thinly sliced scallions, cut on the
   diagonal into long ovals

Up to 2 days before you plan to serve, make the dressing: Heat the oven to 350 degrees. Spread the sesame seeds out on a baking sheet and toast until fragrant, about 15 to 20 minutes, stirring once. Immediately remove the seeds from the baking sheet (they can burn very quickly). When cool, transfer to a blender.

Heat 1 tablespoon peanut oil over medium-high heat. Add the shallots and garlic, and cook, stirring, until softened, 3 to 5 minutes. Let cool slightly and add to the sesame seeds in the blender. Add the remaining 6 tablespoons peanut oil, sesame oil, soy sauce, vinegar, sugar, and sambal, and blend at high speed just until a thick paste forms. Stop blending as soon as most of the seeds have broken up; overprocessing will pulverize all the seeds and make the sauce too oily. *(The recipe can be made up to this point and kept refrigerated up to 2 days.)*

The same day you plan to serve, make the noodles: Bring a large pot of unsalted water to a boil. Gently separate the noodles with your hands and add to the water. Cook until tender (after the water returns to a boil, it will take anywhere from 10 seconds for very thin Chinese noodles to 3 minutes for Italian pasta). Drain the noodles and cool them under cold running water. Drain well. Transfer the cold noodles to a large bowl and toss with the peanut oil.

When ready to serve, remove the dressing from the refrigerator and drain off any oil that has collected on the top. Whisk in about ¾ cup water to thin the dressing and make it creamy; whisk in more a little at a time as needed. Taste for soy sauce, adding more if needed. Whisk in the chopped cilantro. Pour about half of the dressing over the noodles. Add the snow peas, red pepper, and daikon, and toss well to combine (using your hands is easiest). Add the rest of the dressing and finish tossing. Transfer to a large serving bowl or individual plates, garnish with the cilantro leaves, peanuts, and scallions, and serve immediately.

INDIAN VEGETABLE FRITTERS WITH CILANTRO-YOGURT PESTO

MAKES
4 SERVINGS

Simple vegetable fritters (pakoras) are wonderful, and they're even better when the batter has some spice. The trick is in keeping the crust feather-light—with baking powder. Pakoras are popular far beyond India—Singapore, Malaysia, and even New York City. They make perfect appetizers, snacks, side dishes, or even dinner with a substantial salad.

You can use almost any firm vegetable (not tomatoes, for example). Then dip the crisp, hot pakoras in my creamy herbed pesto—though they're very good with plain ketchup, too!

FOR FRYING AND SERVING:
1 cup Indian chickpea flour or whole wheat flour
1 ¼ cups water
½ teaspoon turmeric
½ teaspoon ground cumin
½ teaspoon paprika
½ teaspoon baking powder
Canola oil for frying
Sea salt or kosher salt for sprinkling
Cilantro-Yogurt Pesto (recipe follows)

VEGETABLES (4 CUPS TOTAL):
Cauliflower florets
¼-inch-thick slices of sweet potato
Large rings of onion
½-inch-thick slices of eggplant
½-inch-thick slices of zucchini
Mushroom caps (about 2 inches across)
Scallions (trimmed to about 4 inches long)
Okra, with stems trimmed off

Up to 1 hour before serving, make the batter: Mix the flour with the water, adding more water as needed to make a smooth batter. Mix in the turmeric, cumin, paprika, and baking powder until smooth.

When ready to cook, heat about 1 ½ inches of oil in a deep, heavy pot over high heat until it ripples. Line a cookie sheet with paper towels or brown paper bags. Lower the heat to medium-high. Working in batches to avoid crowding the pot, dip a few vegetables into the batter and slip into the oil. Cook, turning once, until golden brown on both sides, about 2 to 3 minutes total. Firmer vegetables like sweet potatoes and cauliflower will take longer, approximately 4 to 5 minutes, so cook those in separate batches. Lift out with a slotted spoon and drain.

The *pakoras* can be briefly kept warm in a 200-degree oven, but do serve them as soon as possible. Sprinkle with sea salt before serving with cilantro-yogurt pesto.

CILANTRO-YOGURT PESTO

½ cup packed cilantro leaves
2 small jalapeño chiles, stemmed and
    seeded
¼ cup pine nuts
1 clove garlic, chopped

½ cup canola oil
Freshly grated zest of 1 lemon
1 cup thick yogurt (page 9)
Kosher salt and freshly ground black
    pepper

In a food processor or blender, or using a hand blender, puree all the ingredients *except* the yogurt, salt, and pepper together until smooth. Fold in the yogurt and season to taste with salt and pepper. Serve immediately.

Potato Springroll Knishes with Crème Fraîche and Caviar

MAKES
4 to 6
SERVINGS

Both of my hometowns—Kuala Lumpur, where I lived as a child, and New York, where I have lived for many years—have terrific street food. This favorite appetizer from Restaurant AZ combines two of my curbside favorites: crisp, golden Asian springrolls, and knishes filled with mashed potato, grated onion, and a good shot of black pepper. The outsides are wonderfully crisp, and the filling is fluffy and aromatic.

The knishes are delicious plain, and luxurious with a dab of crème fraîche and a few grains of caviar on top. You can buy thin springroll wrappers, made from wheat flour, at Asian markets. They should be about 8 inches square.

1 pound Yukon Gold potatoes, peeled
1 onion, peeled
¾ cup crème fraîche
2 teaspoons salt
1½ teaspoons freshly ground black
   pepper

1 package (about 25) springroll wrappers,
   thawed in the refrigerator if frozen
1 egg, beaten
Canola oil for frying
1 ounce caviar (optional)
Snipped chives, for garnish

Up to 1 day before serving, assemble the knishes: Cover the potatoes with cold salted water, bring to a boil, and boil gently until tender enough to mash smoothly. Grate the onion on the medium holes of a box grater. When the potatoes are cooked, drain well and mash together with the grated onion and ½ cup crème fraîche. Mix in the salt and pepper.

Lay a springroll wrapper on a work surface at an angle so that it looks like a diamond, with one corner pointed toward you. Place a heaping tablespoon of mashed potato just below the center of the diamond. Brush the edges lightly with beaten egg. Fold the top corner down to meet the bottom, making an upside-down triangle (or turnover) shape, and press around the edges to seal. Take the two opposite corners of the triangle and bring them together over the filling. Brush the remaining point of the wrapper (the part that is still lying flat on the counter) lightly with

beaten egg. Now roll the springroll all the way toward you. Set aside and repeat with the remaining ingredients. *(The recipe can be made up to this point and kept refrigerated, uncovered, up to 1 day. Bring to room temperature before continuing.)*

When ready to serve, heat 1 inch of oil in a deep, heavy pot until very hot but not smoking, about 375 degrees. Add a few knishes, not enough to crowd the pan, and fry, turning once or twice, until golden all over, about 1 or 2 minutes total. Remove with a slotted spoon and drain on paper towels. Repeat with the remaining knishes.

Using a serrated knife, cut the knishes across into 2 or 3 pieces. Stand the pieces up on end. Top each piece with a small blob of crème fraîche and a bit of caviar (if using), and sprinkle with chives. Serve immediately.

Ginger-Lacquered Hot Chicken Wings

One of my secret pleasures is Buffalo chicken wings—I can't resist that potent combination of sweet, smoky, and spicy flavors. With their delicious sticky crust, they remind me of another favorite finger food: Chinese barbecued spareribs. I use lots of pineapple, chiles, and ginger in this recipe to make the coating sweet and hot.

At Restaurant AZ, I make this dish from quail and serve it with thin slices of roast pineapple, but it's just as good with celery sticks and fresh blue cheese dressing!

1 ¼ cups pineapple juice
1 cup chopped fresh ginger
  (no need to peel it)
4 dried Thai bird chiles
  (page 2)
2 fresh jalapeño chiles

About 20 chicken wings, pointed tips cut
  off and wings cut in half at the joint
Kosher salt and freshly ground black
  pepper
1 cup rice flour or all-purpose flour
4 cups canola oil

Combine the juice, ginger, dried chiles, and jalapeños in a heavy pot. Simmer until reduced by three-fourths; you should have about ⅓ cup of syrup. Strain out the ginger, chiles, and jalapeños; set the syrup aside in a large mixing bowl. *(The recipe can be made up to this point and kept refrigerated up to 3 days.)*

Pat the wings dry and season with salt and pepper. Dredge lightly with flour.

When ready to serve, heat the oil in a deep, heavy skillet until very hot but not smoking, about 375 degrees. (Or heat the broiler to high.) If you don't have a deep-frying thermometer, test the temperature by tossing in a small piece of bread. If it floats to the top and immediately turns golden brown, the oil is hot enough.

Working in batches to avoid crowding the pan, fry the chicken wings until well browned on both sides, about 5 minutes per batch. Lift the wings out and shake off any excess. (Or broil the wings until crusty, turning once, about 5 minutes.)

Toss the hot wings in the syrup until well coated, then transfer to a serving platter. Repeat with the remaining wings. Serve as soon as possible.

Easy Duck Foie Gras Mousse

MAKES
ABOUT
8 SERVINGS

Somewhere between a French pâté *and Jewish chopped liver, this duck-liver spread is packed with rich flavor. I know it's not especially Asian, but it is everyone's favorite snack in the kitchen at Restaurant AZ. For a delicious contrast, we eat it on slices of grilled bread with whatever pickles happen to be around. The puree is rich and smooth, so crunchy pickles, crisp toast, or celery sticks all make excellent accompaniments.*

¼ cup finely chopped raw bacon
1 large onion, finely chopped
1 ½ pounds duck livers or chicken livers
1 cup Cognac or Armagnac or another
   brandy of your choice
¼ cup ruby port
1 clove garlic, smashed and peeled

2 anchovy fillets
½ to 1 cup crème fraîche
Kosher salt and freshly ground black
   pepper
¼ cup chopped herbs, such as parsley,
   thyme, or chives, *or* a combination
   of the three

Gently cook the bacon in a large, heavy skillet until the fat has rendered and the bacon is crisp and golden brown. Raise the heat and add the onion. Cook, stirring, until the onion is softened and translucent, about 8 minutes. Lift the bacon and onion out of the pan with a slotted spoon, leaving the fat in the pan. Add the duck livers and brown them well all over. Turn off the heat and pour in the brandy and port. Turn the heat back on, bring to a simmer, and cook until the liquids are syrupy, scraping up the browned bits from the bottom of the pan.

    In a mortar and pestle or a food processor, puree the garlic and anchovy together (or mince together until very fine). Add the livers and the liquids from the pan and pulse just until smooth. Place the mixture in a bowl and fold in the bacon and crème fraîche to taste. Season to taste with salt and pepper, and refrigerate until ready to serve. *(The recipe can be made up to this point and kept refrigerated up to 4 days.)*

    Just before serving, taste for salt and pepper and fold in the chopped herbs.

Barbecued Short Ribs with Green Peppercorn–Apple Glaze

No one could love Chinese barbecued spareribs more than I do. They were one of the first classic dishes I set out to rethink for my first restaurant. Short ribs are smaller and more manageable than spareribs, and they have even more delicious meat on them. I make my tangy, spicy-sweet glaze with a combination of apple vinegar and apple jelly, then add briny green peppercorns. Pickled foods such as olives, capers, and peppercorns (not to mention Indian chutneys and Asian pickles) are my favorite easy way to add intense flavor notes in my recipes.

About 5 pounds short ribs, cut into
    2- to 3-inch lengths (ask the butcher
    to do this)
1 (3-ounce) jar green peppercorns in
    brine, drained and coarsely chopped

1 ½ cups apple cider vinegar
3 cups apple jelly or apple butter
1 ½ teaspoons Worcestershire sauce
2 jalapeño chiles, minced

Place the ribs in a large roasting pan. Combine the remaining ingredients in a heavy saucepan and boil until reduced by half.

Heat the oven to 250 degrees. Brush some of the glaze all over the ribs and bake for about 4 hours, until glossy and chewy. Baste with the glaze every 15 minutes or so, or whenever the ribs look dry. Serve warm or at room temperature.

CURRIED LAMB SAMOSAS WITH GRILLED PEACH-MINT *RAITA*

Whether it's called an empanada, *a* knish, *a* pasty, *or a* samosa, *I've never been able to resist a crusty packet of dough stuffed with a savory filling. It's one of my favorite things to eat. This* samosa *has an irresistibly crumbly crust, and the filling explodes with flavor. Whenever I'm lucky enough to have some leftover Roast Boneless Leg of Lamb with Spicy Cumin Crust (page 199), this is how I use it. I love these before a vegetable curry or as a casual dinner with a big salad.*

Traditionally, samosas *are deep-fried, but I find I get excellent (and easier) results from brushing them with butter and baking them instead.*

FOR THE CRUST:
1 cup all-purpose flour
¼ cup Indian chickpea flour or masa harina (Mexican corn flour) or additional all-purpose flour
1 teaspoon kosher salt
4 tablespoons butter, melted

FOR THE FILLING:
1 ¼ cups coarsely ground lamb *or* 1 cup leftover roast lamb, cut into ½-inch dice
2 tablespoons canola oil
1 large onion, chopped
2 cloves garlic, minced
¼ cup minced fresh ginger

4 teaspoons garam masala (page 4)
2 teaspoons curry powder
½ cup baking potatoes, peeled and cut into ½-inch dice
½ cup tomatoes, seeded and cut into ½-inch dice
¾ cup red wine
Kosher salt and freshly ground black pepper
¼ cup chopped cilantro

FOR COOKING AND SERVING:
2 tablespoons butter, melted
Grilled Peach-Mint *Raita* (recipe follows) or Cilantro-Yogurt Pesto (page 45)

Make the crust: In a food processor, combine the flours, salt, and butter, and pulse together. Gradually drizzle in enough water, pulsing between additions, so that the dough forms a ball in the machine. Wrap the dough in plastic wrap and set aside at room temperature for 2 hours.

Meanwhile, make the filling: Heat a large skillet over high heat and add the ground lamb (if using cooked lamb, do not add at this time). Cook, stirring, until browned all over. Remove from the pan with a slotted spoon and wipe out the pan. Heat the oil in the skillet over high heat and add the onions. (If using cooked lamb, begin with this step.) Cook, stirring often, until the onions are well caramelized, meltingly soft, and dark golden brown; this may take up to 25 minutes. Adjust the heat to prevent scorching. When the onions are about 5 minutes away from being fully cooked, add the garlic.

Add the ginger, garam masala, and curry powder, and cook, stirring often, for 5 minutes. Add the cooked lamb, potatoes, and tomatoes, and stir well. Add the wine, bring to a simmer, cover, and simmer for 10 minutes, or until the potatoes are tender. Season to taste with salt and pepper. Set aside to cool, then fold in the cilantro.

Working on a lightly floured surface, pull off a small handful of dough (you should have enough dough to make 12 to 16 handfuls). Roll out each piece of dough into a 5-inch round. Spoon a tablespoon of filling onto the lower half of each round. Lightly wet the edges and lift the upper half of each round up and over the filling, making half-moon-shaped *samosas*. Press to seal and then crimp the edges with the back of a fork. *(The recipe can be made in advance up to this point and kept refrigerated up to 3 days.)*

When ready to cook, preheat the oven to 400 degrees. Arrange the samosas on a well-buttered cookie sheet, brush the tops with melted butter, and bake for 15 to 20 minutes, or until golden brown. Serve hot with cold *raita*.

GRILLED PEACH-MINT RAITA

This cool sauce combines the sweetness of a chutney with the lush creaminess of a raita, yogurt-mint sauces that are drizzled on to tame the fire of hot curries. Cooking the fruit intensifies its sweetness, but feel free to skip this step if you prefer. If you are using a grill and don't want to clean the whole rack, you can instead place the peaches on a wire cooling rack (the kind you'd use to cool warm cookies) and place the wire rack on top of the grill rack.

MAKES
ABOUT
2 CUPS

2 large ripe peaches, peeled, pitted, and
    sliced
Canola oil
1 cup thick yogurt (page 9)

Kosher salt and freshly ground black
    pepper
¼ cup thinly sliced mint leaves

Heat a grill or grill pan until very hot (see note above). Brush the peach slices with oil and place them on the grill. Grill just until softened and caramelized, about 1 minute per side. Let cool.

Dice the peaches and mix them with the yogurt and salt and pepper to taste. Chill until ready to serve, up to 6 hours. Just before serving, fold in the mint.

Small and Main-Course Salads

SIMPLE HERB SALAD WITH SOY-LIME VINAIGRETTE

CUCUMBER, RED PEPPER, AND PEANUT SALAD

CRUNCHY BEAN SPROUT SALAD WITH SESAME AND *SAMBAL*

BALSAMIC-ROASTED CHERRIES AND ARUGULA SALAD

ENDIVE, STILTON, AND ROASTED PEAR SALAD WITH POMEGRANATE VINAIGRETTE

CAESAR SALAD WITH CURED SARDINES AND TINY PICKLED ONIONS

HOT-SMOKED TROUT WITH POTATO-WATERCRESS SALAD AND MUSTARD SEED DRESSING

CRAB AND ASPARAGUS EGG FOO YUNG WITH YUZU-BASIL SALAD

CHILLED "DRUNKEN" CHICKEN WITH THAI GREEN PAPAYA SALAD

SMOKED CHICKEN SALAD WITH HAZELNUTS, MANGO, AND PARSLEY PESTO

SUGAR-CURED BEEF *CARPACCIO* WITH CRUNCHY VEGETABLE SLAW AND LEMONGRASS DRESSING

Simple Herb Salad with Soy-Lime Vinaigrette

I can't imagine what the food at Restaurant AZ would look and taste like without this fragrant toss of green herbs; I top many of my dishes with it. It's somewhere between a garnish and a salad. The mixture adds color, texture, juice, and fragrance to any dish, or it can be expanded into a wonderful salad course all by itself. I wouldn't use the strong "stick herbs" here—such as rosemary, thyme, or marjoram—but any soft herbs can be included. Just make sure that they are very clean and dry. Baby greens like mâche and young watercress flesh out the salad and make it fluffy and crisp, but don't add anything with a tough stem, such as mature arugula or mizuna.

¼ cup parsley leaves
¼ cup cilantro leaves
¼ cup chervil sprigs
¼ cup fennel fronds or additional
  cilantro leaves
¼ cup small basil leaves

½ cup mâche or tender sprouts or
  baby salad greens
½ cup watercress leaves
¼ cup Soy-Lime Vinaigrette
  (recipe follows) or Yuzu Dressing
  (page 73)

Toss the herbs and greens together and keep refrigerated. Just before serving, toss with the vinaigrette.

Soy-Lime Vinaigrette

This light vinaigrette is used in many ways in the kitchen at Restaurant AZ—tossed with sweet microgreens, as a dipping sauce for dumplings, and sprinkled over a bowl of rice with scallions and a succulent piece of broiled fish to make a quick snack in the middle of a shift. It's the variety of flavors that makes it so satisfying—citric, salty, sweet, hot, and toasty.

When someone requests a basic green salad, this is the vinaigrette I always use.

2 tablespoons soy sauce
2 tablespoons freshly squeezed lime juice
1 small pinch of sugar

1 tablespoon dark sesame oil
2 tablespoons canola oil, or to taste
1/2 teaspoon *sambal* (page 8)

Just before serving, whisk all the ingredients together and taste. Add more canola oil if the mixture seems too salty or citric.

CUCUMBER, RED PEPPER, AND PEANUT SALAD

MAKES
4 SERVINGS

A bright, cool cucumber salad is the perfect counterpart to rich curries and hot stir-fries. This one is fresh, spicy, and crisp, and has the surprise crunch of peanuts. The longer you marinate the cucumbers, the more "pickled" they will become, so decide in advance if you want to make a salad or a pickle.

1 long English cucumber or 4 Kirby
    cucumbers, peeled, halved lengthwise,
    seeded, and sliced 1/4 inch thick
1 red bell pepper, seeded and cut into
    matchsticks
1 small jalapeño chile, seeded and minced

1 cup rice wine vinegar
1/2 cup sugar
1/4 cup chopped toasted peanuts
    (page 11)
Whole cilantro leaves, for garnish

Combine the cucumber, red pepper, and jalapeño in a glass or ceramic bowl. Bring the vinegar and sugar to a boil and stir to dissolve the sugar. Pour the hot vinegar over the vegetables. Marinate at least 30 minutes. *(The recipe can be made in advance up to this point and kept refrigerated up to 4 days.)*

    Just before serving, drain off the liquid. Sprinkle with peanuts and cilantro, and serve.

CRUNCHY BEAN SPROUT SALAD WITH SESAME AND *SAMBAL*

Soybean sprouts, with their pale greenish heads, are even crunchier than the usual white sprouts (from mung beans). I like to spark their mild flavor with classic seasonings of the Southeast Asian kitchen: soy, lime, shallot, chile, sesame, and sugar. Somehow all those disparate flavors come together in the perfect, light, crisp accompaniment for any rich dish, especially those with coconut such as my Spicy Coconut Soup with Shellfish, Fresh Herbs, and Noodles (page 138) or Malaysian Beef Rendang (page 189).

The soybean sprouts need to be blanched to remove their raw texture, but don't cook them.

1 pound soybean sprouts (available at
    Asian markets)
⅓ cup soy sauce
¼ cup freshly squeezed lime juice
1 shallot, minced

2 tablespoons *sambal* (page 8)
2 tablespoons sugar
2 tablespoons dark sesame oil
¼ cup canola oil

Blanch the bean sprouts in a large pot of boiling water for 30 seconds. Drain.

In a large bowl, whisk the remaining ingredients together. Add the sprouts and toss well. Marinate at least 30 minutes. *(The recipe can be made in advance and kept refrigerated up to 2 days.)*

Just before serving, drain off the liquid.

Balsamic-Roasted Cherries and Arugula Salad

SPRING/SUMMER

Juicy red cherries, creamy snow-white cheese, and peppery green arugula make up my own take on the familiar colors of a tomato-mozzarella-basil salad. I can't seem to resist putting fruit in my salads, probably because its sweetness is so pleasing with a few drops of vinaigrette. The effect is rather like an Indian chutney. Roasting the cherries with balsamic vinegar makes them soft and tangy, the better to contrast with the mild farmer cheese.

2 cups pitted fresh cherries (use Bing cherries for the best color)
2 tablespoons chopped shallots
½ cup balsamic vinegar
¼ cup canola oil
Kosher salt and freshly ground black pepper

½ cup olive oil
1 teaspoon Dijon mustard
¼ cup farmer cheese
2 tablespoons heavy cream
4 to 6 cups arugula
8 slices sourdough bread

Heat the oven to 500 degrees. In a small roasting pan, toss the cherries, shallots, vinegar, and canola oil together. Season with salt and pepper, and roast until the cherries start to blister and soften, about 10 minutes.

Lift the cherries out of the pan with a slotted spoon and reserve. Pour the pan juices into a bowl and whisk in the olive oil and mustard. Season to taste with salt and pepper.

Mix the farmer cheese with the cream.

When ready to serve, place the arugula in a large bowl. Toast the bread. Toss the arugula with some of the vinaigrette (the greens should be evenly but lightly coated) and season to taste with salt, pepper, and more vinaigrette if needed. Divide the greens among the serving plates and sprinkle cherries on top. Spread the toast with the cheese mixture and divide among the plates.

Endive, Stilton, and Roasted Pear Salad with Pomegranate Vinaigrette

FALL / WINTER

My favorite dishes, whether they're Chinese, Mediterranean, Indian, or (like this one) French in origin, are those where lots of flavors and textures come together. I adore this classic combination of slightly bitter endive spears; crunchy, warm-flavored walnuts; and creamy, pungent blue cheese from the French southwest. I like to add the sweetness of pears, concentrating their flavor and texture by roasting them. And instead of plain vinegar in the dressing, I use tangy-sweet pomegranate molasses, a concentrated juice used in Middle Eastern kitchens, to layer even more flavor into the finished salad.

If you can't find the small pears called Seckel pears, in season in the fall, choose slightly underripe Bosc pears, the kind with the brown skin.

FOR THE PEARS:

15 Seckel pears, peeled, halved, and cored, or 6 Bosc pears, peeled, halved, cored, and thickly sliced
½ cup honey
¼ cup brandy, apple cider, or apple cider vinegar
2 tablespoons melted butter

FOR THE WALNUTS:

1 cup walnut pieces
¼ cup dark brown sugar
2 teaspoons to 1 tablespoon pure chile powder, such as ancho, or cayenne pepper
1 tablespoon kosher salt

TO FINISH THE SALAD:

½ cup apple cider vinegar
1 cup canola oil
½ cup extra-virgin olive oil
Kosher salt and freshly ground black pepper
6 endives
4 cups watercress leaves, mâche, or another crisp salad green
½ cup crumbled Stilton, Roquefort, or another pungent blue cheese

Heat the oven to 350 degrees. Toss the pears, honey, brandy, and melted butter in a roasting pan and bake about 30 minutes, stirring once, until the pears are tender and caramelized. Let cool, reserving any liquid in the pan.

Meanwhile, prepare the walnuts: Bring a saucepan of water to a boil. Blanch the walnuts in the water for 2 minutes, then drain well (this step helps to make the coating adhere, but it is optional). Mix the sugar, chile powder, and salt together, and toss the walnuts in the mixture. Spread the nuts out on a sheet pan. Place in the 350-degree oven (you can bake them at the same time as the pears) and bake until the nuts are toasted and the coating melts, 10 to 15 minutes.

Make the dressing: Set aside 12 pear pieces for the salad. Combine the remaining pears, their liquid, the vinegar, and the oils in a blender and puree until smooth and emulsified. Season to taste with salt and pepper.

Just before serving, separate the endive leaves and slice them crosswise into strips. Place the endives, watercress, and walnuts in a salad bowl and top with the remaining pear pieces. When ready to serve, whisk the dressing together and pour half of it over the salad. Toss well and taste; add more dressing as needed. Divide the salad among serving plates and sprinkle each serving with blue cheese.

Caesar Salad with Cured Sardines and Tiny Pickled Onions

I've always been fascinated by the unlikely combination of flavors that makes Caesar salad so deliciously popular—it's lemony, cheesy, fishy, and garlicky all at once. I've incorporated all those flavors into my version, but tweaked some of the ingredients. Asian fish sauce replaces the usual Worcestershire sauce (which is made of anchovies and soy sauce, among other things). Instead of lemon juice and anchovies, I make a little seviche of sardines, marinating them in lemon juice until firm and tender. The sardines also make the salad more substantial; it makes a good lunch or summertime main course. You can start with fresh sardine fillets or cured ones from a gourmet store, or you can leave them out altogether.

I love the richness of Caesar dressing, but sometimes it can be so thick that it weighs down the greens. To prevent that, I replace some of the oil in my dressing with buttermilk. Finally, since I can't resist adding a tangy element to a rich dish, I toss in a few crisp pickled onions; they, too, are entirely optional.

FOR THE ONIONS (OPTIONAL):
1 cup peeled fresh or frozen pearl onions or thinly sliced onions
1 cup apple cider vinegar
½ cup sugar
1 tablespoon turmeric

FOR THE SARDINES (OPTIONAL):
1 onion, thinly sliced
1 bulb fennel, thinly sliced
12 fresh sardines, filleted (your fish market can do this), or canned white anchovies, available at gourmet stores
Freshly squeezed juice of 4 lemons
Kosher salt and freshly ground black pepper

FOR THE SALAD:
2 to 3 heads romaine lettuce, dark outer leaves discarded
1 egg yolk (omit if salmonella is a concern in your area)
Freshly grated zest and freshly squeezed juice of 1 lemon
1 clove garlic, finely minced
1 anchovy fillet, finely minced, or 1 tablespoon fish sauce (page 3)
1 tablespoon coarse-grain mustard
1 cup canola oil
¼ cup buttermilk
1 cup freshly grated Parmesan cheese

Prepare the onions: Place the onions in a bowl. Combine the vinegar, sugar, and turmeric in a saucepan and bring to a boil over medium heat. Strain the mixture through a coffee filter (to remove the turmeric) into the bowl containing the onions. Let pickle at least 1 hour (30 minutes for sliced onions). Store in the liquid. *(The recipe can be made up to this point and kept refrigerated indefinitely.)*

At least 1 day before serving, prepare the sardines: In the bottom of a wide, shallow bowl, spread a layer of onion and fennel slices. Cover with a layer of sardine fillets and season well with salt and pepper. Repeat with the remaining onion, fennel, and sardines. Pour lemon juice over the layers, cover, and refrigerate for at least 8 hours and up to 24 hours. Remove and reserve the sardines; discard the vegetables and marinade.

Make the salad: Separate the leaves of the lettuce and wash and dry well. Tear any large leaves into manageable pieces, but keep the inner leaves whole. Refrigerate until ready to serve.

When ready to serve, make the dressing: Whisk the egg yolk until smooth and pale yellow. Whisk in the lemon zest and juice, garlic, anchovy, and mustard. Whisk in the oil a few tablespoons at a time. Once all the oil is incorporated, whisk in the buttermilk and ¾ cup of cheese. Season to taste with salt, pepper, and fish sauce.

To serve, toss the lettuce with some of the vinaigrette (the greens should be evenly but lightly coated). Add more vinaigrette to taste and divide on serving plates. Garnish with sardines and onions, sprinkle with the remaining cheese, and serve.

HOT-SMOKED TROUT WITH POTATO-WATERCRESS SALAD AND MUSTARD SEED DRESSING

Smoking fish is really much easier than you might think, and the results are just ex-traordinary. I like to use a nice fatty sea trout called steelhead for smoking because the fat helps the fish absorb the flavors. This salad, based on a classic English plate of smoked fish and watercress, has my additions of pungent mustard, floury potatoes, and fresh herbs, plus the crunch of tart apple. (Beet slices can be alternated with the potato, for color.) It's very delicious and easy—especially if you buy your smoked trout from my favorite supplier, the Browne Trading Company (see Sources, page 233).

If you don't have a smoker, you can easily improvise one with a heavy pot with a tight-fitting lid. Or use a heavy roasting pan and cover it with several layers of alu-minum foil. You'll also need a rack that fits inside the pan to place the trout on.

FOR THE TROUT:

1 ½ pounds fresh trout fillets, preferably
   steelhead (see note above)
½ cup plus 2 tablespoons dark brown
   sugar
½ cup kosher salt
1 cup raw rice
2 pods star anise
2 cinnamon sticks, about 3 inches long

FOR THE SALAD:

4 large boiling potatoes, preferably Yukon
   Gold, peeled
2 cups watercress, thick stems removed
½ cup parsley
½ cup chopped tarragon
½ cup chopped chives
2 shallots, minced
¼ cup coarse-grain mustard
½ cup olive oil
Kosher salt and freshly ground black
   pepper
1 tart apple such as Granny Smith, peeled
   and cut into matchsticks
Freshly squeezed juice of 1 lemon
Watercress sprigs, for garnish

Prepare the trout: Rinse the trout and pat dry. Mix ½ cup sugar and salt together, and gently pack the mixture on the fillets. Let cure for 30 to 60 minutes, then

rinse off the curing mixture. Pat the fillets dry and arrange them on a rack that fits in the smoking pan.

Line the smoking pan with 2 layers of aluminum foil. Mix the remaining 2 tablespoons sugar, rice, and spices together, and spread out the mixture in the lined pan. Place the pan over high heat until the mixture starts to smoke. Remove from the heat, place the trout on the rack in the pan, and cover the whole thing tightly. Return the pan to the stove over high heat. Smoke the trout for 5 minutes for rare fish. (If you like your fish cooked through, don't just leave it in the smoker for longer, continue the cooking by placing the trout on a baking sheet and baking at 325 degrees about 5 minutes more.) Let cool. *(The recipe can be made in advance up to this point and kept refrigerated up to 1 week.)*

Cut the trout fillets into pieces for serving.

Make the salad: Steam or boil the potatoes until tender all the way through, approximately 15 minutes to boil and 25 minutes to steam. While they are still hot, slice them thin and place them in a bowl.

Coarsely chop the watercress and parsley. Whisk the tarragon, chives, shallots, mustard, and oil together. Mix in the watercress and parsley and pour the dressing over the hot potatoes. Toss well and season to taste with salt and pepper. Set aside at room temperature to let the potatoes absorb the dressing. Just before serving, gently mix in the apples and lemon juice.

To serve, place a piece of trout on a serving plate, then add a layer of potato salad. Top with another piece of trout and garnish with watercress sprigs.

CRAB AND ASPARAGUS
EGG FOO YUNG WITH
YUZU-BASIL SALAD

Some people say that egg foo yung isn't "real" Chinese cooking, but my Chinese grandmother always made this simple dish for us kids when the grown-ups were eating something unappetizing. For a while this category included all green vegetables, so I ate a lot of egg foo yung, and over the years it came to taste like everything comforting and savory. I still love it, and the first time I tasted an Italian frittata I recognized a close cousin. Like a frittata, this can be served either hot or at room temperature.

Crab, asparagus, and mushrooms make a wonderful combination of flavors and textures, but you can add almost anything you like. Eggs and basil have a natural affinity, so the peppery leaves of basil in my citrusy salad really pull the dish together. It makes a great lunch or brunch entrée.

1 tablespoon plus 4 teaspoons canola oil
1 clove garlic, minced
1 cup asparagus, cut into 1-inch lengths
   and blanched in boiling water until
   bright green and just cooked through
1 cup mushrooms, preferably shiitake,
   thinly sliced

12 eggs
1 cup lump crabmeat, picked over for bits
   of shell and cartilage
1 teaspoon fish sauce (page 3)
Kosher salt and freshly ground black
   pepper
Yuzu-Basil Salad (recipe follows)

Heat 1 tablespoon oil in a large nonstick skillet over high heat. Add the garlic, asparagus, and mushrooms, and cook, stirring, until fragrant and golden, about 5 minutes. Transfer to a large bowl and wipe out the pan.

When the mushroom mixture is almost cooled to room temperature, lightly beat the eggs together. Add to the mushroom mixture along with the crabmeat, fish sauce, and salt and pepper to taste. Mix well.

Heat the oven to 400 degrees (or, if your broiler is in the oven, heat it to medium-high). Heat 2 teaspoons of remaining oil in the skillet over high heat. Pour in half of the egg mixture (make sure you get half of the "goodies" on the bottom) and immediately reduce the heat to low and cook without disturbing for 4 to 5 minutes. Transfer the pan to the top rack of the oven and cook 3 minutes more, until the egg is puffed and set (this will take less time under the broiler). Slide the egg foo yung out of the pan onto a plate and set aside. Repeat with the remaining egg mixture and oil.

Cut into wedges and serve warm or at room temperature with Yuzu-Basil Salad.

Yuzu-Basil Salad

The yuzu dressing, with its delicate citrus perfume, is a personal favorite. It is wonderfully useful and, depending on how much mustard you use, can be strong or gentle in flavor. With my Simple Herb Salad (page 58), I use less or no mustard to show off the flavors of the herbs; for a crunchy lettuce salad, I prefer a more assertive dressing. It also makes a wonderful splash for plain grilled or broiled fish.

A yuzu is a small Japanese citrus fruit; it is too sour to eat but has a fragrant juice and zest. The frozen juice is available from Katagiri (see Sources, page 233) and other Japanese vendors.

FOR THE YUZU DRESSING:
1/2 cup yuzu juice (see note above) or
   2 tablespoons *each* fresh lemon juice,
   lime juice, orange juice, and grapefruit
   juice
1 shallot, minced
2 tablespoons Dijon mustard, or less to
   taste
1 cup extra-virgin olive oil
Kosher salt and freshly ground black
   pepper

FOR THE SALAD GREENS:
Leaves of 1 medium bunch basil (don't
   use very large leaves or ones with black
   spots)
6 to 8 cups mixed salad greens, such as
   Boston, watercress, or other mild
   greens

Whisk the yuzu juice, shallot, and mustard together. Whisk in the oil, salt, and pepper to taste.

Just before serving, whisk the dressing together and pour a few tablespoons over the basil and greens. Toss to coat. Taste and add more dressing as needed.

CHILLED "DRUNKEN" CHICKEN WITH THAI GREEN PAPAYA SALAD

Drunken chicken—that is, steamed chicken marinated in rice wine and other delicious aromatics—is a classic Chinese banquet dish. It is usually the first dish on the menu, since it's light and savory and not too filling. That is also what makes it perfect as a chicken salad. I like to pair the velvet-soft, ginger- and soy-flavored chicken pieces with a crisp citrusy salad made of green papaya.

I've included instructions for poaching the chicken, but it can also be steamed for 50 minutes if you have a large enough steamer.

1 small (2½-pound) chicken
3 tablespoons Szechuan pepper salt (page 13)
2 quarts lightly salted Chicken Stock (page 13)
1 cup rice wine (page 7)

1 tablespoon soy sauce
1 tablespoon ginger juice (page 4)
2 scallions, chopped
Thai Green Papaya Salad (recipe follows)
Cilantro sprigs, for garnish

Rub the chicken inside and out with the pepper salt. Cover and refrigerate at least 1 hour or up to 4 hours. Bring the stock to a simmer in a pot just large enough to hold the chicken snugly. Add the chicken, cover, and cook at a bare simmer for 40 to 45 minutes. Let cool in the broth until cool enough to handle, then drain (keep the stock for another purpose, such as soupmaking).

Meanwhile, mix the rice wine, soy sauce, ginger juice, and scallions together. Remove the meat from the bones, shred it into bite-size pieces, and place in a bowl. Pour the marinade over the warm chicken. Marinate in the refrigerator for at least 24 hours.

Drain off the excess liquid before serving with Thai Green Papaya Salad. Garnish with cilantro sprigs.

THAI GREEN PAPAYA SALAD

MAKES
4 SERVINGS

Thai green papaya salad is one of my favorite dishes, a riot of big flavors: garlic, fresh chiles, peanuts, cilantro, and fresh lime juice. Shredded green (unripe) papaya is the salad's main ingredient, but it's there for crunch and juice and adds little flavor; it is rather like the iceberg lettuce of Southeast Asia. You can buy green papayas in any Chinatown market or substitute one small head of cabbage, finely shredded.

4 tablespoons canola oil (if using shrimp)
1 tablespoon dried shrimp, soaked and
    drained (optional; see page 8)
1 green papaya, peeled and seeded (see
    above)
2 cloves garlic, smashed and peeled
2 small fresh chiles, such as jalapeño,
    Fresno, or serrano

¼ cup chopped tomatoes
2 tablespoons fish sauce (page 3)
2 teaspoons sugar
Freshly squeezed juice of 1 lime, or more
    to taste
¼ cup chopped roasted peanuts
¼ cup cilantro leaves

Heat the oil in a small skillet over high heat. Add the shrimp and cook, stirring, until browned and fragrant. Drain and set aside to cool, then chop coarsely.

Cut the green papaya into matchsticks or grate coarsely in a food processor. Using a mortar and pestle or a food processor, pound or pulse the garlic, chiles, and tomato together. Mix in the dried shrimp, fish sauce, sugar, and lime juice. Toss with the green papaya. *(The recipe can be made in advance up to this point and kept refrigerated up to 1 hour.)* Just before serving, taste for lime juice and sprinkle with peanuts and cilantro.

SMOKED CHICKEN SALAD WITH HAZELNUTS, MANGO, AND PARSLEY PESTO

This salad is all about showing off the glorious toasty flavor of hazelnuts, a favorite of mine. Everything goes with them—fresh green herbs, pungent cheese, sweet juicy fruit, and smoked chicken. The combination of the crunchy nuts and aromatic hazelnut oil is intoxicating. All together, the salad explodes with textures and tastes, and the mild spark of vinegar brings out the individual ingredients.

FOR THE PESTO:
½ cup hazelnuts, toasted (page 11)
2 cups parsley leaves
½ cup grated Parmesan cheese
1 cup hazelnut oil (available at gourmet
  markets)
Kosher salt and freshly ground black
  pepper

FOR THE CHICKEN SALAD:
4 smoked chicken breast halves or
  1 ½ pounds smoked or roasted chicken
  or turkey

6 to 8 cups cooked penne pasta, rinsed,
  tossed with 2 teaspoons canola oil, and
  kept at room temperature
2 small oranges, peeled, seeded, and
  segmented
1 mango, peeled, pitted, and diced
2 tablespoons white wine vinegar or rice
  wine vinegar
2 endives, leaves separated
1 head butter, Bibb, or Boston lettuce,
  with leaves separated

Combine the hazelnuts, parsley, and cheese in a food processor. Pulse together until the nuts and parsley are coarsely ground. Add the oil and process until well combined. Season to taste with salt and pepper.

Toss the chicken, penne, oranges, mango, and vinegar with some of the pesto (you may have more pesto than you need). Taste and add more pesto as needed. Toss well, transfer to a shallow serving bowl, and surround the salad with endive spears and lettuce leaves.

Sugar-Cured Beef Carpaccio with Crunchy Vegetable Slaw and Lemongrass Dressing

This is an elegant, unusual, and extremely tasty salad. My easy salt-and-sugar cure draws moisture out of a juicy beef tenderloin, leaving it smooth, silky, and with a peppery aftertaste and a prosciutto-like flavor and texture. Maybe that's why it's so good with a soft fruit like persimmon, if you can find it, or mango. As in Italian prosciutto-and-melon, the sweet, juicy fruit really brings out the flavor of the meat.

If uncooked beef does not appeal to you, you can still serve this dish. Increase the amount of tenderloin to 2 pounds. Follow the curing instructions, letting the meat absorb the cure for about 36 hours, and then slice the tenderloin into individual filet mignons. Grill or sear them for a great entrée.

FOR THE BEEF:
1 pound beef tenderloin in one piece
¼ cup kosher salt
¼ cup medium- or coarse-ground black
    pepper
1 pound palm sugar (page 8) or dark
    brown sugar

FOR THE SALAD:
1 cup green papaya or jicama, cut into
    matchsticks
½ cup carrots, cut into matchsticks
½ cup seeded cucumber, cut into
    matchsticks
½ cup celery, cut into matchsticks
½ cup red bell pepper, cut into
    matchsticks
½ cup *each* shredded mint, cilantro, and
    basil
½ cup Lemongrass Dressing (recipe
    follows)
Freshly squeezed juice of 2 limes
1 large, ripe Fuyu persimmon or mango or
    peach, diced
Mint, cilantro, and basil sprigs, for garnish

Up to 10 days before serving, cure the beef: Rinse the beef and pat dry. Rub it with the salt and 2 tablespoons pepper. Pack all the sugar onto the beef and wrap it tightly in plastic wrap. Refrigerate at least 24 hours and up to 36 hours. Rinse off the curing mixture. Pat the meat dry and rub with the remaining 2 tablespoons pepper. Refrigerate until ready to serve, up to 10 days.

When almost ready to serve, make the salad: Toss all the vegetables and herbs together. Toss with the dressing and lime juice, then set aside for 15 minutes.

Slice the chilled beef into paper-thin slices (it's easiest to cut it cold, right when it comes out of the refrigerator). Place a mound of salad in the center of a serving plate, then drape a few slices of the beef over the salad. Place persimmon pieces around each mound and garnish with herb sprigs.

LEMONGRASS DRESSING

1 stalk lemongrass, tough top and bottom
   parts trimmed off and discarded
2 cloves garlic, peeled
2 (¼-inch) slices ginger (do not peel)
1 shallot, coarsely chopped

1 jalapeño chile, coarsely chopped
½ cup sugar
¼ cup fish sauce (page 3)
Freshly squeezed juice of 2 limes
About ½ cup canola oil

Slice the lemongrass thin and place in a food processor. Add the garlic and ginger, and pulse just until coarsely ground. Add the shallot and jalapeño, and process until finely ground.

Pour the sugar into a medium-size heavy saucepan and turn the heat to medium-high. Cook, breaking up any lumps with a wooden spoon, until the sugar melts and turns amber, about 5 minutes. Add the lemongrass mixture and cook for 1 minute, stirring constantly (the mixture will seize up at first and then smooth out). Carefully pour in the fish sauce and simmer to blend, about 30 seconds. Remove from the heat and let cool to room temperature. When cooled, whisk in the lime juice and then the oil to taste. Use immediately or cover and refrigerate up to 1 week. Season to taste with fish sauce and lime juice right before serving.

Soups

CHILLED ASPARAGUS SOUP WITH
CRABMEAT SALAD

SWEET TOMATO-RED PEPPER SOUP WITH
GARLIC CREAM

CHILLED WHITE CORN SOUP WITH
SCALLOP SEVICHE

TANGY SWEET POTATO SOUP WITH
COCONUT MILK

CREAMY LENTIL, FENNEL, AND SPICE SOUP

KABOCHA SQUASH AND CHESTNUT SOUP
WITH CHIPOTLE CREAM

HOT AND SOUR SOUP WITH SEVEN
TREASURES

CORN AND PEEKYTOE CRAB CONGEE

CURRIED CAULIFLOWER SOUP WITH CILANTRO
CRÈME FRAÎCHE

CRAB AND ASPARAGUS EGG-DROP SOUP

Chilled Asparagus Soup with Crabmeat Salad

SPRING/SUMMER

Sweet crabmeat with tender green vegetables is a classic springtime combination in Chinese cooking. My rendition is this smooth, fresh soup that makes use of every bit of the asparagus stalk. A quick simmer in chicken stock makes the woody bottoms give up their essence, intensifying the asparagus flavor of the finished soup. A spoonful of lemony crab salad adds luxury and a briny freshness to each bowl, but feel free to serve the soup plain.

You may wonder why this soup, unlike most, is chilled before it's pureed. That's because chilling the asparagus as soon as possible after cooking helps set the bright green color.

FOR THE SOUP:
2 bunches asparagus
4 cups (1 quart) lightly salted Chicken Stock (page 13) or canned broth
3 tablespoons butter
1 onion, chopped
2 leeks (white part only), well washed and chopped
2 stalks celery, chopped
2 russet baking potatoes, peeled and roughly chopped
1 cup crème fraîche
Kosher salt and freshly ground black pepper

FOR THE CRAB SALAD:
1 cup lump crabmeat, picked over for bits of shell and cartilage
1 shallot, minced
2 tablespoons minced garlic chives or regular chives
Freshly grated zest of 1 lemon
Salt and freshly ground black pepper
Freshly squeezed lemon juice

At least 6 hours or up to 1 day before serving, make the soup: Snap off the woody bottoms of the asparagus (they will naturally break at the point where they become woody) and reserve. Cut off the tips and reserve. Cut the remainder of the spears into 1/2-inch lengths.

In a medium pot, bring the stock to a simmer. Add 12 (or 2 per serving) asparagus tips and cook for 1 minute. Remove with a slotted spoon and set aside. Add the woody asparagus bottoms to the stock and simmer for 15 minutes. Lift the asparagus bottoms out of the stock and discard them.

In another deep pot, melt the butter. When it foams, add the onion, leeks, and celery, and cook, stirring, until the onion is softened and translucent (do not brown), about 10 minutes. Add the potatoes and stock, and simmer until the potatoes are almost tender, about 10 minutes. Add the sliced asparagus and the remaining raw asparagus tips, and cook until the asparagus is very tender, about 3 to 5 minutes more.

As soon as possible, transfer the soup to the refrigerator. Chill until very cold, about 4 hours or overnight. Puree the chilled soup with a hand blender or in batches in a blender, then strain into a serving bowl. Stir in the crème fraîche and add salt and pepper to taste. Keep cold.

Make the crab salad: Gently stir the crab, shallot, chives, and zest together. Add salt and pepper to taste and squeeze in a little lemon juice to moisten the mixture.

To serve, ladle the soup into bowls, then carefully place a large spoonful of crab salad in the center of each serving. Top the salad with 2 of the blanched asparagus tips. Serve immediately.

CHILLED WHITE CORN SOUP WITH SCALLOP SEVICHE

SUMMER

If you like a cool, creamy vichysoisse on a hot day, I know you'll love this soup. With the silkiness of corn added, it's summery, sweet, and refreshing. Making a broth from the corn cobs is a very easy way of packing even more corn flavor into each bowl.

When you're serving cold soup, it's especially important to add a tart note to wake up the flavors. I love corn and shellfish together, so a lime juice–spiked seviche is perfect. But just a last-minute squeeze of lime juice would be good, too.

FOR THE SEVICHE:
8 ounces bay scallops or sea scallops
   (cut sea scallops into quarters)
1 small red onion, chopped
1 jalapeño chile, seeded and chopped
Freshly squeezed juice of 1 lemon
Freshly squeezed juice of 1 lime
Freshly squeezed juice of 1 orange
2 tablespoons sugar
Kosher salt and freshly ground black
   pepper
¼ cup chopped cilantro

FOR THE SOUP:
6 cobs white corn
4 cups (1 quart) lightly salted Chicken
   Stock (page 13) or canned broth
4 tablespoons unsalted butter
1 small onion, chopped
1 medium Yukon Gold potato, peeled
   and roughly chopped
1 cup white wine
Kosher salt and freshly ground black
   pepper
Freshly squeezed lemon juice

At least 2 hours or up to 24 hours before serving, make the seviche: Combine the scallops, onion, jalapeño, citrus juices, and sugar in a glass or stainless bowl. Refrigerate, stirring occasionally. The scallops will turn white and firm. Just before serving, drain off any liquid and add salt and pepper to taste. Fold in the cilantro.

At least 6 hours or up to 24 hours before serving, make the soup: Cut the corn kernels off the cobs. Place the cobs in a large pot and reserve the kernels separately. Add the stock to the corn cobs and bring to a boil over high heat. Lower the heat and simmer for 5 minutes. Lift out the cobs and discard; reserve the stock.

Melt the butter in a medium pot. When it foams, add the onion and reserved corn kernels, and cook, stirring, until the onion is softened and translucent. Add the chopped potato and wine, and simmer until most of the liquid has evaporated. Add the stock and simmer until the potatoes are tender, about 10 minutes. Let cool slightly, then puree with a hand blender or in batches in a blender. If you like, strain the soup to make it even smoother. Add salt, pepper, and lemon juice to taste. Chill until very cold.

When ready to serve, taste the soup for salt, pepper, and lemon juice. Ladle into bowls, then carefully place a large spoonful of seviche in the center of each serving. Serve immediately.

CREAMY LENTIL, FENNEL, AND SPICE SOUP

This very easy basic is one of my favorite soups of all time. I think it's the combination of delicate fennel and strong spice that I love. To emphasize the fennel flavor, I use both fennel seeds and fresh fennel. It's both soothing and stimulating, and the lentils provide great body while the wine and tomatoes add a note of acidity.

2 tablespoons canola oil
1 fennel bulb, diced
1 onion, chopped
1 clove garlic, minced
2 tablespoons garam masala (page 4)
2 tablespoons fennel seeds, toasted and
    ground (page 12)
1 cup diced tomatoes

1 cup yellow lentils (page 5)
1 cup white wine
3 cups lightly salted Chicken Stock
    (page 13), vegetable stock, or canned
    broth
Salt
Crème fraîche and cilantro leaves,
    for garnish

Up to 3 days before serving, make the soup: Heat the oil in a large pot over high heat. Add the diced fennel, onion, and garlic, and cook, stirring, until softened and fragrant, 8 to 10 minutes. Add the garam masala, ground fennel, and tomatoes. Cook, stirring often, about 10 minutes. Add the lentils and wine, and simmer 10 minutes, stirring occasionally.

Pour in the stock and simmer until the lentils are very tender, 20 to 30 minutes more. The soup can be served immediately or cooled slightly and pureed until smooth with a hand blender (or in batches in a blender). (*The recipe can be made in advance up to this point and kept refrigerated up to 3 days.*)

Just before serving, reheat the soup and taste for salt. Top each bowl with a small dollop of crème fraîche and a few cilantro leaves.

Hot and Sour Soup with Seven Treasures

MAKES
8 TO 10
SERVINGS

I can't remember a time when I didn't have a passion for hot and sour soup. Sometimes I think that the soup's special combination of hot, sour, earthy, smoky, sweet, and spicy flavors had a profound influence on me; as a chef, many of my dishes combine all those flavor elements. I love piling ingredient after ingredient into a soup, making it almost a meal in itself. If you prefer to add other "treasures," such as bamboo shoots, feel free to do so; but remember that odd numbers are always luckier in Chinese astrology!

Black vinegar, made from sticky rice, is a precious seasoning in the Chinese kitchen, but I get very good results with balsamic vinegar as a substitute.

2 tablespoons canola oil
½ cup minced fresh ginger
½ cup minced shallots
½ cup minced garlic
3 quarts Double-Chicken Broth (page 144), Chicken Stock (page 13), or canned broth
24 small dried tree ear mushrooms, soaked in hot water for 30 minutes and drained
16 large shrimp, peeled, deveined, and halved lengthwise
1 cup shredded cooked chicken (such as the chicken from making Double-Chicken Broth, or leftover roast chicken)
1 cup shredded roast duck or additional chicken

¼ cup lily buds (available at Asian markets), soaked in warm water until soft
½ cup thinly sliced fresh shiitake mushrooms, with stems removed and discarded
½ cup thinly sliced sugar snap or snow peas
1 cup Chinese black (Chinkiang) vinegar *or* ¼ cup balsamic vinegar
2 tablespoons *sambal* (page 8), or to taste
Fish sauce (page 3)
Kosher salt and freshly ground black pepper
Finely shredded scallions, for garnish

Heat the oil in a large, heavy pot over high heat. Add the ginger, shallots, and garlic, and cook, stirring, until softened and translucent, 8 to 10 minutes. Add the stock and bring to a boil. Just before serving, add all the remaining ingredients and simmer until the shiitake mushrooms are cooked. Add fish sauce, salt, and pepper to taste. Taste for *sambal* (the "hot") and vinegar (the "sour"). Serve hot, sprinkled with shreds of scallion.

Curried Cauliflower Soup with Cilantro Crème Fraîche

Spicy, moist cauliflower curries are very popular in India. In this recipe you're simply brewing up an earthy cauliflower curry, then blending it into a soup with stock and spiking it with cool cream. Raw cauliflower is tough and cabbagey, but the florets become silky soft and surprisingly sweet with slow braising and absorb spices beautifully. Another reason I love to cook with cauliflower is that it's available all year round; this soup is equally as good hot for a winter dinner as it is chilled on a summer picnic.

MAKES
6 SERVINGS

2 tablespoons canola oil
1 head cauliflower, trimmed and roughly chopped into 2-inch pieces
1 onion, chopped
2 teaspoons chopped fresh ginger
2 teaspoons garam masala (page 4)
2 potatoes, peeled and roughly cut into ½-inch pieces

2 quarts lightly salted Chicken Stock (page 13), vegetable stock, or canned broth
Kosher salt and freshly ground black pepper
1 cup cilantro leaves
¼ cup crème fraîche

Make the soup: In a medium pot, heat the oil and add the cauliflower, onion, and ginger. Cook over medium heat, stirring, until softened, about 10 to 15 minutes. Raise the heat to high and add the garam masala. Cook, stirring constantly, until the mixture is fragrant and lightly browned, 3 to 5 minutes. Add the potatoes and stock, and simmer until the potatoes and cauliflower are tender, about 15 minutes. Using a hand blender or working in batches in a blender, puree the soup until smooth. (If you like a very smooth soup, strain it into a clean pot.) Season to taste with salt and pepper. *(The recipe can be made in advance up to this point and kept refrigerated up to 3 days.)*

Make the cilantro crème fraîche: Place the cilantro in a blender and add a dollop of crème fraîche. Puree, adding more crème fraîche if necessary. When smooth, transfer to a serving bowl and stir in the remaining crème fraîche. Keep refrigerated.

To serve, reheat and taste for salt and pepper. Top with a dollop of crème fraîche.

SWEET TOMATO-RED PEPPER SOUP WITH GARLIC CREAM

MAKES
6 SERVINGS

SUMMER

This fire-engine red soup is incredibly bright—in color and in flavor. The two vegetables balance each other out, with the peppers adding sweetness to the tomatoes, and the tomatoes sparking the peppers with a little acid. To round the flavors, I use the richness of anchovy fillets, but you won't even taste them in the finished soup. (I promise!)

The finished soup has the vegetable freshness of gazpacho and is excellent hot or cold. This unctuous warm garlic cream is my favorite way to show off the delirious perfume of garlic.

FOR THE SOUP:
2 tablespoons canola oil
1 large onion, diced
2 cloves garlic, smashed
1 teaspoon hot red pepper flakes
2 anchovy fillets, minced
4 red bell peppers, seeded and roughly
   chopped
4 cups diced fresh tomatoes (no need to
   peel them) or drained canned tomatoes
1 cup lightly salted Chicken Stock (page
   13) or vegetable stock, or water
10 whole basil leaves
About 2 tablespoons balsamic vinegar
About ¼ cup extra-virgin olive oil
   (optional)
Kosher salt and freshly ground black
   pepper

FOR THE CREAM:
1 cup heavy cream
6 cloves garlic, peeled and smashed
¼ cup freshly grated Parmesan cheese

Make the soup: In a large, heavy pot, heat the oil over medium-high heat. Add the onions, lower the heat to medium, and cook slowly, stirring often, until the onions are soft, about 15 minutes. Add the garlic, red pepper flakes, anchovies, and peppers. Raise the heat and cook, stirring, until fragrant. Add the tomatoes and stock, and simmer for 1 hour, fishing out the garlic cloves after 30 minutes if you prefer a less garlicky flavor.

Turn off the heat and stir in the basil leaves. Let rest for 30 minutes at room temperature to infuse the flavor, then remove the basil and discard. Using a hand blender or working in batches in a blender, puree the soup until smooth. Strain the soup into a clean pot. Season to taste with balsamic vinegar, olive oil, salt, and pepper. *(The recipe can be made in advance up to this point and kept refrigerated up to 3 days.)*

Make the garlic cream: Combine the cream and garlic in a saucepan and simmer until the garlic is soft and tender, about 15 to 20 minutes. Turn off the heat and remove the garlic. Whisk in the cheese.

To serve, reheat the soup and taste again for seasonings. Top each bowl with a drizzle of garlic cream.

Tangy Sweet Potato Soup with Coconut Milk

If you like creamy squash soup or Thai coconut soup—or both, as I do—you'll adore this soup immediately. It's a Southeast Asian classic and almost ridiculously easy to make, but the flavors are layered and complex. Coconut milk makes soups taste rich and smooth, a perfect foil for the tang of lime juice and fish sauce. The combination of roasted squash and sweet potatoes is silkier than sweet potatoes alone. And fresh cilantro leaves and chopped peanuts add a final texture twist.

1 medium-size (about 1 ½ pounds) kabocha squash, butternut squash, or pumpkin, *or* 24 ounces canned unsweetened pumpkin puree
1 pound sweet potatoes, peeled and cut into 2-inch chunks
2 cups lightly salted Chicken Stock (page 13) or canned broth
1 (14-ounce) can coconut milk
1 stalk lemongrass, tough ends trimmed off and discarded, and smashed in a few places with the handle of a knife

2 kaffir lime leaves (page 4) or 2 teaspoons freshly grated lime zest
2 tablespoons freshly squeezed lime juice
1 tablespoon fish sauce (page 3)
Kosher salt
Chopped roasted peanuts and whole cilantro leaves, for garnish

Heat the oven to 350 degrees.

Place the whole squash in the oven and bake about 50 minutes, until the flesh feels very tender when you press the skin. Let cool, then cut in half. Scoop out and discard the seeds (or set them aside to toast later) and scoop the flesh out of the skin. Discard the skin and reserve the flesh. (If using canned puree, skip this step.)

Meanwhile, combine the sweet potatoes, stock, and coconut milk in a soup pot. Bring to a simmer and add the lemongrass and lime leaves, if using (if using lime zest, do not add it yet). Simmer for 30 minutes, until the potatoes are tender.

Add the reserved squash to the pot. Remove the lemongrass and lime leaves.

Using a hand blender or working in batches in a blender or food processor, puree the soup until smooth. *(The recipe can be made in advance up to this point and kept refrigerated up to 1 day.)*

Just before serving, reheat the soup and thin it with more stock if necessary. Season to taste with lime juice, fish sauce, salt, and lime zest, if using. Sprinkle each bowl with peanuts and cilantro.

KABOCHA SQUASH AND CHESTNUT SOUP WITH CHIPOTLE CREAM

MAKES
8 SERVINGS

FALL/WINTER

I've always loved smoky flavors, and when I was introduced at my first cooking job to Mexico's chipotle chiles (by a young chef named Bobby Flay), it was love at first taste. Chipotles are simply smoked jalapeños. Chipotles preserved in adobo (the kind you buy in cans) are spicy, smoky, tangy, and sweet all at once. They make a wonderful counterpoint to the delicate flavor of kabocha, a mild, smooth-textured squash that is popular in Japanese cooking. The combination is a perfect fall or winter first course.

I deepen the chipotles' flavor by stirring them with concentrated port wine and tomato paste (the tartness and sweetness both pick up the flavors) and then with crème fraîche for a cooling effect.

FOR THE CHIPOTLE CREAM:
1 cup ruby port
½ cup dry red wine
1 teaspoon chipotles in adobo or crushed dried chipotles
2 tablespoons tomato paste
1 cup crème fraîche or sour cream

FOR THE SOUP:
2 (2½-pound) kabocha, acorn, or butternut squash, halved crosswise and seeded
2 quarts lightly salted Chicken Stock (page 13) or canned broth
10 ounces whole chestnuts, roasted and peeled (available in jars at the supermarket during the holidays or at a gourmet market any time of year)
2 tablespoons pure maple syrup
Kosher salt and freshly ground black pepper

Make the cream: Combine the port, red wine, chipotles, and tomato paste in a saucepan and bring to a boil. Lower the heat and simmer until reduced to a thick paste, about 12 minutes. Transfer to a bowl to cool. When cool, fold in the crème fraîche and refrigerate until ready to serve. *(The recipe can be made in advance up to this point and kept refrigerated up to 3 days.)*

Make the soup: Heat the oven to 350 degrees. Oil a baking sheet and place the squash halves, cut side down, on the sheet. Bake until soft, about 1 hour. When cool enough to handle, scoop the squash out of their skins. Measure about 6 cups of squash and transfer to a large pot. (Save any remaining squash for another use.)

Add the stock and chestnuts, and bring to a boil over high heat. Lower the heat and simmer, uncovered, until the chestnuts are soft, about 30 minutes. Stir in the maple syrup. Using a hand blender or working in batches in a blender, puree the soup until very smooth, then return to the pot. Add salt and pepper to taste. *(The recipe can be made in advance up to this point and kept refrigerated up to 1 day.)*

Reheat the soup before serving. Taste for salt and pepper. Drizzle each serving with chipotle cream.

CORN AND PEEKYTOE CRAB CONGEE

SUMMER

Congee is probably the most popular Chinese dish that Americans have never heard of. It is rice that is boiled and boiled until very smooth and soupy (a bit like cream of rice cereal), and it is eaten all over China for breakfast, lunch, and sometimes even dinner. The flavor is mild and (to my mind, since I love plain rice) delicious, but it is what you put on the congee that makes the dish.

To transform my favorite congee into a delicate soup, I cook the rice in a quick, super-flavorful stock made from corn cobs (the corn kernels go in later). I stir in some briny-sweet crabmeat. And then just before serving, I spike each bowl with fish sauce, scallions, and toasty sesame oil.

10 ears fresh corn
4 cups (1 quart) lightly salted Chicken Stock (page 13) or canned broth
1 cup arborio or other risotto rice
1 tablespoon fish sauce (page 3), plus extra for garnish

Kosher salt and freshly ground black pepper
1 cup lump crabmeat, picked over for bits of shell and cartilage
2 to 4 scallions, sliced on the diagonal into thin ovals
1 tablespoon dark sesame oil

Cut the corn kernels off the cobs. Place the cobs in a large pot and reserve the kernels separately. Add the stock to the corn cobs and bring to a boil over high heat. Lower the heat and simmer for 5 minutes. Lift out the corn cobs and discard.

Add the rice to the hot stock and simmer, stirring often, until the rice is very soft, 15 to 20 minutes. Add the corn kernels and simmer 5 minutes more. Using a hand blender or working in batches in a blender, puree the soup until smooth. *(The recipe can be made in advance up to this point and kept refrigerated up to 2 days.)*

Just before serving, reheat the soup and season to taste with fish sauce, salt, and pepper. Stir in the crabmeat and serve, garnishing each serving with scallions, a drop of fish sauce, and a drizzle of sesame oil.

CRAB AND ASPARAGUS EGG-DROP SOUP

SPRING/SUMMER

Egg-drop soup is the most comforting home-cooking soup I know, quickly made by stirring a beaten egg into a whirlpool of hot stock. It is delicate and nourishing, and I like to dress it up in springtime, when asparagus is at its peak, with slivers of bright green asparagus and flakes of rich crabmeat.

To help the egg form nice long ribbons, whisk a tablespoon of the stock with the egg before adding it. This breaks down the proteins of the egg and keeps it from stiffening in the hot soup.

2 teaspoons canola oil
½ cup thinly sliced shallots
2 tablespoons thinly sliced garlic
1 cup thinly sliced asparagus stalks
   (reserve the asparagus tips separately)
4 cups (1 quart) lightly salted Chicken
   Stock (page 13) or canned broth
½ pound lump crabmeat, picked over for
   bits of shell and cartilage (optional)

2 teaspoons fish sauce (page 3)
Kosher salt and freshly ground black
   pepper
1 egg, beaten
1 tablespoon chopped cilantro
Whole cilantro leaves and finely shredded
   scallions, for garnish

Heat the oil in a medium-size soup pot over medium-high heat. Add the shallots and garlic, and cook, stirring, until softened; do not brown. Add the asparagus stalks and stir to coat with the oil. Add the stock and bring to a boil, then lower the heat and simmer for 5 minutes. Turn off the heat and stir in the crabmeat. Season to taste with fish sauce, salt, and pepper.

Just before serving, bring the soup to a simmer and add the asparagus tips. Cook for 1 minute. Whisk 1 tablespoon of hot soup into the egg (see note above). While stirring the soup, drizzle in the beaten egg. Stir in the chopped cilantro and serve, garnished with cilantro leaves and shreds of scallion.

Fish and Shellfish Main Courses

HALIBUT STEAMED IN SOY-GINGER BROTH
WITH MUSHROOMS AND CHINESE SAUSAGE

PAN-CRISPED BASS FILLETS WITH *UMEBOSHI*
PLUM SAUCE AND GINGERED HASH BROWNS

ROASTED ROUGET WITH THAI GREEN CURRY
SAUCE AND SPICY-SWEET MANGO SALAD

SESAME-CRUSTED STURGEON WITH TART
PLUM SAUCE AND MISO-GLAZED EGGPLANT

BROILED SALMON, ONION-SESAME STICKY
RICE, AND SPICED SOY DRIZZLE

CRISPED SALMON PACKETS WITH AROMATIC
TOMATO–BLACK BEAN SAUCE AND THAI RICE
NOODLE SALAD

CRISPY TUNA *MAKI* WITH VEGETABLE SLAW
AND SWEET GINGER DRESSING

CORIANDER-CRUST TUNA WITH GINGER-
ORANGE–BRAISED OXTAIL

CURRIED MONKFISH "OSSO BUCO" WITH
SLOW-ROASTED TOMATOES AND CAULIFLOWER
COUSCOUS

SEARED SCALLOPS WITH WASABI CUCUMBER
SALAD AND PORT GLAZE

STIR-FRIED EGG NOODLES WITH SHRIMP AND
SHIITAKE MUSHROOMS

SAMBAL-GRILLED SHRIMP WITH MINTED
SOYBEAN WONTONS AND TOMATO WATER

THAI *BOUILLABAISSE* WITH BLACKFISH,
MUSSELS, CLAMS, AND SPINACH

SPICY COCONUT SOUP WITH SHELLFISH,
FRESH HERBS, AND NOODLES

Halibut Steamed in Soy-Ginger Broth with Mushrooms and Chinese Sausage

MAKES
4 SERVINGS

Steamed fish is true Chinese home cooking. It's firm, hearty, and delicate, the better to contrast with lively aromatics such as ginger, soy, and scallions. In this dish I invented a way to use aromatics for texture as well as flavor—matchsticks of ginger, bits of Chinese dried sausage, and even ripe, sweet plum tomatoes. I like to rest my fish fillets on a pillow of soft tofu that combines with the soy broth to bathe everything in a lovely sauce. Serve this on top of fluffy rice to absorb the liquids.

Like lemon or lime in Western kitchens, ginger is almost always included in Asian recipes for fish.

FOR THE BROTH:
½ cup soy sauce
¼ cup fish sauce (page 3)
½ cup plum wine (page 6)
1 cup water
1 tablespoon sugar
2 cloves garlic, minced
2 jalapeño chiles, minced
2 inches fresh ginger, peeled and minced

FOR THE FISH:
2 (about 4-inch-square) blocks soft tofu, cut into 2-inch-wide strips
4 (6-ounce) fillets of halibut or another white, firm fish such as cod
2 plum tomatoes, finely diced
2 Chinese sausages (page 8), cut into matchsticks
2 knobs Szechuan mustard (page 6), cut into matchsticks (optional)
10 fresh shiitake mushrooms, stems removed and caps thinly sliced
2 scallions, white parts only, thinly sliced into rings
2 tablespoons fresh ginger, peeled and cut into matchsticks
Cilantro sprigs, for garnish

Combine all the ingredients for the broth and stir until the sugar dissolves. Set aside. *(The broth can be made in advance and kept refrigerated up to 1 week.)*

Set up a large bamboo steamer or improvise one using a large pot with a tight-

fitting lid: Pour 1 inch of water into the bottom of the pot. Place 1 or more small heatproof dishes (such as ramekins) in the bottom to prop up the baking dish.

Arrange the tofu in a baking dish small enough to fit in the steamer. Arrange the fish fillets on top of the tofu. Evenly sprinkle the tomatoes, sausages, mustard, mushrooms, scallions, and ginger over the top.

When ready to cook, bring the water in the steamer to a boil. Drizzle ¼ cup of broth over the top of the fish and place the dish in the steamer. Cook about 15 to 20 minutes, or until the fish in the middle of the dish flakes slightly under pressure (you'll have to move the aromatics aside to press the fish). Serve immediately, garnished with cilantro sprigs. Pass the remaining broth at the table.

Pan-Crisped Bass Fillets with *Umeboshi* Plum Sauce and Gingered Hash Browns

Flaky, crisped fillets of white fish; lightly gingered and golden brown cubes of potato; a tangy-sweet sauce with a faint perfume of plums—this dish is a perfect orchestration of flavors and textures. The ginger and garlic in the hash browns really tie the fish and potatoes together.

And then there's the extraordinary sauce. Pickled plums (umeboshi) are soft, deep purple-red, and more salty than sweet; they are part of the large family of Japanese pickles. A little bit of umeboshi goes a long way; I modify their punch by pureeing them with honey, soft vinegars, and a neutral oil. The result is a sweet, tart, and prettily pink vinaigrette with an addictive flavor that is perfect with fish.

FOR THE SAUCE:
1 (12-ounce) jar *umeboshi* plums, drained
   and pitted (see Sources, page 233)
¼ cup red or white wine vinegar
¼ cup rice wine vinegar
4 tablespoons honey
1 cup canola oil

FOR THE FISH:
2 tablespoons canola oil
1 tablespoon butter
4 (6-ounce) sea bass fillets with skin on
   or thin fillets of another white, firm fish
Finely shredded scallions, for garnish

Make the sauce: Combine the plums, vinegars, and honey in a blender. Puree until smooth. Gradually drizzle in the canola oil, blending until the mixture emulsifies. Taste, adding more oil if needed. Set aside. *(The recipe can be made in advance up to this point and kept refrigerated up to 3 days.)*

Just before serving, cook the fish: Preheat the oven to 400 degrees. Heat a heavy skillet (preferably cast iron) over high heat for 2 minutes. Add the oil and butter, and swirl until the butter melts and the foam has subsided. Place the fish in the pan, skin side down, and lower the heat to medium. Let cook for 2 minutes undisturbed, then transfer to the oven (don't turn the fish over). Bake 3 minutes more or longer, until done to your liking. Serve drizzled with plum sauce and garnished with shreds of scallion.

Gingered Hash Browns

This is a very crisp and fragrant variation on an American classic. Ginger and potatoes are an unexpected combination that is especially wonderful with fish or steak dishes.

3 cups Yukon Gold potatoes, peeled and
   cut into ½-inch dice
2 tablespoons canola oil
2 tablespoons butter
2 tablespoons minced garlic
2 tablespoons minced fresh ginger

2 tablespoons chopped dried shrimp
   (page 8; optional)
1 or 2 jalapeño chiles, minced
Kosher salt and freshly ground black
   pepper

Boil the potatoes just until tender but not mushy, about 5 to 10 minutes. Drain well.

Heat the oil and butter in a heavy skillet over high heat. When the butter melts and the foam has subsided, add the garlic, ginger, shrimp, and jalapeño, and cook, stirring, just until softened, about 2 minutes. Add the potatoes, lower the heat to medium, and gently brown the potatoes on all sides, stirring occasionally.

Season to taste with salt and pepper. Serve immediately.

Roasted Rouget with Thai Green Curry Sauce and Spicy-Sweet Mango Salad

MAKES
4 TO 6
SERVINGS

Thai curry pastes, pounded together from an astounding assortment of chiles, spices, and aromatics, are great examples of how much fun it is to layer flavor upon flavor until you have a wildly delicious sauce for something simple like grilled chicken or, in this case, roasted fish. Green curry paste is based on fresh green chiles, shallots, and cilantro (red curry paste is based on dried red chiles, and yellow curry paste on fresh turmeric). Spices such as cumin, coriander, clove, and nutmeg are woven in as well.

I've applied the classic French method of saucemaking to those lively ingredients, brewing them together and then straining out the aromatics. The brew is fiery, but I mellow it back down with coconut milk to make a smooth, rich pale green sauce. Drizzled over snowy fillets, the sauce practically sings on the plate. If it seems too spicy, try an old chef's trick: Whisk in a few tablespoons of cold butter.

FOR THE SAUCE:
2 teaspoons canola oil
I onion, diced
I carrot, diced
I apple, peeled and diced
½ cup minced fresh ginger (unpeeled okay)
2 jalapeño chiles
2 stalks lemongrass, tough ends trimmed off and discarded, smashed with the handle of a heavy knife
2 kaffir lime leaves (page 4) or 2 teaspoons freshly grated lime zest
I tablespoon Thai green curry paste (page 4; optional)
I cup rice wine (page 7)
2 cups lightly salted Shellfish Stock (page 15) or clam juice

I cup coconut milk
2 poblano chiles, roasted, peeled, and seeded (page 10)
I cup chopped cilantro
2 tablespoons fish sauce (page 3), or to taste
Freshly squeezed lime juice
Salt

TO FINISH THE DISH:
8 to 12 small rouget fillets or 2 pounds snapper, trout, or sole fillets, skin on
¼ cup Lemongrass Oil (recipe follows)
Kosher salt and freshly ground black pepper
Spicy-Sweet Mango Salad (recipe follows)
Cilantro sprigs and finely shredded scallions, for garnish

FISH AND
SHELLFISH
MAIN
COURSES

Make the sauce: Heat the oil in a medium-size heavy saucepan over medium-high heat. Add the onion, carrot, apple, ginger, jalapeños, and lemongrass, and cook, stirring, until softened and fragrant. Add the lime leaves (if using zest, do not add it at this time) and curry paste, and cook until very fragrant. Add the rice wine and cook until the liquid has evaporated. Add the stock and coconut milk, and boil until reduced by half. Strain the sauce into a clean saucepan or a blender; discard the vegetables. Add the poblanos and cilantro. Using a hand blender if possible, or working in batches in a blender, puree the sauce until very smooth. Season to taste with fish sauce, lime juice (and lime zest, if using), and salt. Keep warm.

Just before serving, cook the fish: Heat the oven to 400 degrees. Toss the fish fillets in the lemongrass oil and season generously with salt and pepper. Arrange the fillets in a single layer in a roasting pan and roast for 5 to 7 minutes, or until done to your liking. Serve immediately, drizzled with green curry sauce and with mango salad on the side. Garnish with cilantro sprigs and shreds of scallion.

Lemongrass Oil

MAKES
½ CUP

Lemongrass is indeed a grass and not a citrus fruit at all, but its scent comes from the same chemical compounds found in lemon zest. It's one of the signature flavors of Southeast Asian cooking. It can be very strong (in fact, lemongrass is closely related to citronella), so I cut it with kaffir limes. Kaffir limes themselves are too knobby and pithy to use in cooking, but the dried leaves of the tree, rather like bay leaves, impart their floral fragrance. The result is a long-lasting oil imbued with lemon and lime flavors.

2 stalks lemongrass, tough ends trimmed   ½ cup canola oil
    off and discarded
5 kaffir lime leaves (page 4), minced, or
    zest of 3 limes

Mince the lemongrass stalks and place in a bowl or glass jar with the lime leaves. Add the oil and let sit at least 2 hours or up to 12 hours. After 12 hours, strain out the lemongrass and lime leaves, and refrigerate the oil. Will keep indefinitely.

SPICY-SWEET MANGO SALAD

This salad is where the American Southwest and Southeast Asia, two of my favorite culinary regions, meet to celebrate the flavors of mangoes, limes, and chiles. It's both a juicy salad and a sweet-hot salsa. I love the pink, green, orange, and red color palette.

2 ripe mangoes, peeled and diced
1 red onion, diced
1 red bell pepper, seeded and diced
1 jalapeño chile, minced

Freshly squeezed juice of 1 lime
2 teaspoons canola oil
Kosher salt and freshly ground black
    pepper

Just before serving, toss all the ingredients together. Season to taste with salt and pepper and serve.

Sesame-Crusted Sturgeon with Tart Plum Sauce and Miso-Glazed Eggplant

I like fish fillets to have a crisp, super-crunchy crust, so I was extremely excited when I devised this foolproof method. I make a quick paste in the food processor to slather all over the fish, then roll it in lots of sesame seeds. The seeds adhere to the mousse much more effectively than to bare fish. I chose sturgeon here for its rich but mild flavor and meaty texture, but you can use any fish you like.

Instead of the usual citrus or ginger for contrast, in this recipe I make a sweet, tart, aromatic sauce based on umeboshi (Japanese pickled plums) and sweet plum wine. It's great with the smooth, delicate fish, toasted sesame seeds, and steamed rice.

FOR THE SAUCE:
2 tablespoons canola oil
½ cup pitted *umeboshi* plums (see Sources, page 233), coarsely chopped
2 pitted fresh plums, coarsely chopped
1 shallot, minced
½ cup lightly salted Chicken Stock (page 13), Shellfish Stock (page 15), or canned broth
¼ cup plum wine (page 6)
¼ cup rice wine vinegar
2 tablespoons honey
¼ cup dark sesame oil
Kosher salt

FOR THE FISH MOUSSE:
4 ounces skinless cod fillets or raw shrimp or raw scallops
1 egg white
2 tablespoons heavy cream *or* lightly salted Chicken Stock (page 13) or Shellfish Stock (page 15)

¼ teaspoon finely minced fresh ginger
¼ teaspoon finely minced scallion, white part only
Fish sauce (page 3)
Kosher salt and freshly ground black pepper

TO FINISH THE DISH:
6 (6-ounce) sturgeon fillets, about 1 ½ inches thick
¼ cup white sesame seeds, toasted (page 12)
¼ cup black sesame seeds, toasted (page 12)
⅓ cup canola oil
Miso-Glazed Eggplant (recipe follows)
Cilantro sprigs and finely shredded scallions, for garnish

Make the sauce: Heat the oil in a skillet over medium-high heat. Add both kinds of plums and the shallot, and cook, stirring, until soft. Add the stock and wine, and simmer for 5 minutes. Add the vinegar and honey, and simmer 5 minutes more. Let cool slightly. Using a hand blender or blender, puree until smooth. Whisk in the sesame oil and season to taste with salt.

Make the fish mousse: In a food processor, pulse the fish a few times to break it up. Add the egg white and cream, and puree until smooth and incorporated. Fold in the ginger and scallion, and season to taste with fish sauce, salt, and pepper.

When ready to cook, rinse the fish and pat dry (the drier the fish, the better the mousse will stick). Combine both kinds of sesame seeds in a shallow bowl. Smear a thin coat of mousse all over a sturgeon fillet (coating the top, bottom, and sides) and roll it in the sesame seeds. Set aside and repeat with the other fillets.

Heat the oven to 350 degrees. Heat the oil in a deep, heavy skillet. Place the fillets in the oil and lower the heat to medium (the oil should be bubbling gently around the fillets so that the sesame seeds toast but do not burn). Cook until the sesame seeds turn golden brown, about 1 ½ minutes per side. Turn the fish to cook on both sides. Transfer the fish to an ovenproof dish and bake about 7 minutes more, until cooked through in the center. Let cool 1 minute before serving (the sesame seeds will be very hot). Serve drizzled with plum sauce and with miso-glazed eggplant on the side. Garnish with cilantro sprigs and shreds of scallion.

Miso-Glazed Eggplant

This is an easy and classic Japanese preparation for eggplant. The nutty tang of miso makes the eggplant taste rich and earthy. Instead of using plain miso, I cut it with salty hoisin and spicy chile sambal for extra flavor, and I use the sweetness of plum wine to tame the bitter edge that eggplant can have.

Small Japanese eggplants are less spongy than the big Italian ones and have fewer seeds. To choose the eggplants with the fewest seeds, pick male ones rather than female. It's easy to tell the difference: At the base, male eggplants have a long groove, and female ones have a dimple.

1 cup *shiro* miso, also known as sweet or
   blond miso (page 6)
½ cup hoisin sauce (page 4)
½ cup rice wine (page 7)
2 teaspoons *sambal* (page 8)
½ cup plum wine (page 6)

1 cup canola oil, plus extra for grilling
12 medium-size Asian eggplants (page 3)
Sesame seeds, toasted (page 12), for
   garnish

Whisk the miso, hoisin, rice wine, *sambal*, plum wine, and canola oil together and set aside. About 30 minutes before cooking, peel the eggplants and cut them in half. Toss the eggplant halves in about half of the glaze and marinate about 30 minutes.

Meanwhile, heat a grill, grill pan, or heavy skillet until very hot (the eggplant may also be broiled). Brush the pan with a little canola oil and add the eggplant in a single layer. Cook the eggplant about 5 minutes per side, lowering the heat to prevent burning and basting every few minutes with the remaining glaze. Serve hot or at room temperature, sprinkled with sesame seeds.

BROILED SALMON, ONION-SESAME STICKY RICE, AND SPICED SOY DRIZZLE

I think of this simple dish as my "giant sushi" entrée. Each serving looks like an over-grown piece of sushi—a pillow of rice with a nice chunk of fish on top. The salmon is broiled and then drizzled with my version of smoky-sweet teriyaki sauce, rather like the barbecued eel, or unagi, you may have tasted at Japanese restaurants. The cool crunch of cucumber tames the heat of the sauce, rounding out all the textures and flavors. If you like, serve it with a dab of wasabi, Japanese horseradish that you can buy in a tube, and shreds of juicy pickled ginger.

FOR THE DRIZZLE:
1 cup soy sauce
1 pound dark brown sugar
4 Thai bird chiles (page 2)
1 cinnamon stick, about 3-inches long
2 star anise

FOR THE MARINADE:
¼ cup sugar
¼ cup hot water
1 cup *shiro* miso, also known as sweet or
    blond miso (page 6)
¼ cup mirin (page 5)
¼ cup rice wine (page 7)

TO FINISH THE DISH:
Onion-Sesame Sticky Rice (recipe
    follows)
6 (6-ounce) salmon fillets, about
    1½-inches thick
1 Kirby cucumber, very thinly sliced
Finely shredded scallions, for garnish

Make the drizzle: Combine all the ingredients in a saucepan and simmer until reduced to about ¼ cup. Strain, discarding the spices. *(The drizzle can be made in advance and kept refrigerated up to 1 month.)*

Make the marinade: Whisk together the sugar, water, miso, mirin, and rice wine. *(The marinade can be made in advance and kept refrigerated up to 1 week.)*

Form the sticky rice into rectangles slightly longer and thicker than the salmon

pieces so that when the salmon rests on the rice, the whole thing will look like a giant piece of sushi.

About half an hour before serving, place the salmon in the marinade. Heat the broiler to very hot or heat a grill pan or heavy skillet brushed with a little canola oil. Cook for 3 minutes per side for medium-rare fish (my favorite). (If you prefer your fish more cooked, transfer the fish to a preheated 350-degree oven and bake up to 5 minutes more.)

Arrange a layer of cucumber rounds on each plate. Divide the fish on rectangles of sticky rice and arrange on the plates. Add the drizzle, garnish with shreds of scallion, and serve.

ONION-SESAME STICKY RICE

MAKES
6 SERVINGS

Japanese sushi rice is short grain, cooked until tender, and just a bit sticky so that it holds together when you lift a piece of sushi to your mouth. It's also seasoned with a bit of tangy rice vinegar. I like to punch up the flavor of the rice in this simple dish. While the rice is cooking, I use the time to slowly caramelize some onions. Then I stir them in along with a drizzle of sesame oil. The heat of the rice releases all of its nose-filling fragrance.

1 ½ cups short-grain rice (page 7)
2 ½ cups water
3 tablespoons canola oil
1 cup minced onion

2 teaspoons dark sesame oil, or to taste
Szechuan pepper salt (page 13)

Rinse the rice for 1 minute under cold running water. Transfer it to a heavy saucepan with a tight-fitting lid and add the water. Bring to a boil, uncovered, over high heat. When the mixture boils, stir to dislodge any grains that are sticking to the pot. Turn the heat to very low and cover tightly. Cook for 25 minutes, then turn off the heat and, without removing the lid, let sit for 10 minutes.

Meanwhile, heat the canola oil in a heavy skillet over high heat. Add the onion and cook until golden brown, lowering the heat to prevent scorching, and stirring often, approximately 30 minutes. Stir the onion into the cooked rice and season the mixture to taste with sesame oil and pepper salt.

CRISPED SALMON PACKETS WITH AROMATIC TOMATO–BLACK BEAN SAUCE AND THAI RICE NOODLE SALAD

MAKES
4 TO 6
SERVINGS

One of my missions as a chef is to make salmon—always the most popular fish on the menu—interesting again. To create this fabulous entrée, I attack the project from two directions. First, I brew up a chunky sauce of tomatoes, black beans, ginger, chiles, and garlic. It tastes like a savory marriage of Mediterranean tomato sauce and Chinese black bean sauce. (It's also wonderful on pasta, by the way.) Then I give the salmon a crisp golden crust by wrapping each fillet in translucent rice paper. It's very thin and cooks up beautifully in the frying pan.

The dish comes together with flaky fish, a crisp crust, a savory sauce, and a cool, fresh-tasting noodle salad. The salmon and sauce would also be great with my Thai Green Papaya Salad (page 75) or your favorite vegetable slaw.

FOR THE SAUCE:
2 tablespoons Chinese fermented
    black beans (page 1)
¼ cup canola oil
¼ cup minced shallots
2 tablespoons minced fresh ginger
2 tablespoons minced jalapeño chiles
2 cups diced tomatoes
1 tablespoon tomato paste
2 tablespoons dark brown sugar
1 cup white wine
1 cup lightly salted Shellfish Stock
    (page 15), Chicken Stock (page 13),
    or water
Kosher salt and freshly ground black
    pepper
Sherry vinegar (optional)

TO FINISH THE DISH:
1½ to 2 pounds (6 ounces per person)
    salmon fillets, cut into 2-ounce pieces
Freshly ground black pepper
1 (12-ounce) bottle of beer, any kind
2 tablespoons sugar
2 tablespoons salt
12 pieces rice paper (page 7)
¼ cup canola oil
Cilantro sprigs and finely shredded
    scallions, for garnish
Thai Rice Noodle Salad (recipe follows)

Make the sauce: Soak the black beans in 1 cup boiling water for 10 minutes. Heat the oil in a medium-size heavy saucepan over high heat. Add the shallots, ginger, and jalapeño, and stir. Drain the black beans and add them to the pot. Cook, stirring, for 5 minutes, lowering the heat to prevent scorching. Add the tomatoes,

tomato paste, and brown sugar, raise the heat, and cook until the mixture is soft and fragrant, about 5 minutes. Add the white wine and simmer until reduced by half, scraping up any browned bits from the bottom of the pan. Add the stock and simmer until reduced by about one-fourth to a chunky sauce. Season to taste with salt, pepper, and sherry vinegar, if using. (If your tomatoes are less than perfect, you may also need to add a pinch or two of sugar to bring out the flavor.) *(The sauce can be made up to 8 hours in advance.)*

Make the packets: Rinse the salmon fillets and pat dry. Season well with pepper. In a large saucepan over low heat, combine the beer, sugar, and salt, and stir to dissolve the sugar. Heat until warm. Lightly dampen a clean lint-free towel and lay it on a work surface. Dip a piece of rice paper into the warm beer mixture until softened and very slightly tacky, then lay it out on the towel at an angle, so that it looks like a diamond. (The towel will absorb any excess liquid.) Place a piece of salmon in the center. Fold the top corner over the fish. Fold in the sides, then fold up the bottom, completely enfolding the salmon in a rice paper package. Set aside, seam side down, and repeat with the remaining ingredients. Refrigerate, covered lightly with a towel, until ready to serve. *(The packets can be made up to 12 hours in advance.)*

When ready to serve, heat 1 inch of canola oil in a deep, heavy skillet over high heat. Working in batches to avoid crowding the pan, add the packets and cook on each side until the rice paper turns crisp and golden brown, about 2 to 3 minutes per side. You can keep the packets warm in a 200-degree oven ready to serve, which should be as soon as possible. To serve, spoon the hot sauce onto plates. Place 3 packets on top and garnish with cilantro sprigs and shreds of scallion. Serve rice noodle salad on the side.

THAI RICE NOODLE SALAD

MAKES
4 SERVINGS

This addictive salad doesn't look like much—and then you taste it. The flavor punch is in the dressing, a pureed mixture of chiles, ginger, and garlic cooked with shallots and curry powder. It's all tossed with slim, light rice noodles, lots of lime juice, and Thai fish sauce. The dried shrimp add a certain richness and texture, but the salad is also good without them. It's wonderful with things like crisp fish, fried chicken, and grilled shrimp, so I usually make a double batch.

8 ounces thin rice stick noodles
   (page 7)
Canola oil or Scallion Oil (page 12)
½ cup dried shrimp, rehydrated and
   drained (page 8)
2 cloves garlic
¼ cup minced fresh ginger
1 or 2 minced jalapeño chiles

½ cup thinly sliced shallots
1 teaspoon curry powder
Freshly squeezed juice of 2 limes, or more
   to taste
2 tablespoons fish sauce (page 3),
   or more to taste
¼ cup chopped cilantro
1 large red bell pepper, diced

Bring a large pot of water to a boil. Add the rice sticks, stir well, then turn off the heat. Let soak for 10 minutes, then drain and transfer to a large bowl. Toss with a little oil to prevent sticking.

Meanwhile, place the drained dried shrimp in a blender. Add the garlic, ginger, and jalapeño, and puree. Heat ½ cup oil in a large skillet over high heat. Add the shallots and cook, stirring, until softened and lightly browned. Add the shrimp mixture and curry powder. Cook, stirring, until well blended, golden, and fragrant. Pour over the noodles and toss very, very gently to avoid breaking up the noodles. If possible, let cool and then toss the salad together with your hands. *(The recipe can be made up to this point and kept up to 4 hours. Do not refrigerate.)*

Just before serving, toss with lime juice, fish sauce, cilantro, and bell pepper. Taste for lime juice and fish sauce, and serve.

CRISPY TUNA MAKI WITH VEGETABLE SLAW AND SWEET GINGER DRESSING

MAKES
4 TO 6
SERVINGS

These tuna rolls are even more irresistible than the sushi maki *that everyone loves. Instead of rolling my tuna in seaweed, I roll it in cracked pepper, then dip it into a tempura batter and fry it up quickly for the crispiest, fluffiest crust. My version of the spicy mayonnaise served at sushi bars is this creamy ginger dressing. I toss it with shreds of fresh vegetables to make a sharp, sweet, crunchy vegetable slaw that's perfect with the mouthfuls of fried fish. You can make the slaw well in advance, but cook the tuna just before serving. Serve rice alongside if you like.*

FOR THE VEGETABLE SLAW:
½ cup drained and finely chopped
    Japanese pickled ginger
2 tablespoons rice wine vinegar
1 teaspoon sugar
1 cup mayonnaise
1 cup *each* matchstick-size pieces of
    cucumber, Napa cabbage, carrots, and
    red bell pepper

FOR THE TEMPURA BATTER:
1 cup all-purpose flour
1 tablespoon baking powder
1½ cups cold club soda
Kosher salt and freshly ground black
    pepper
2 egg whites, whipped to soft peaks

FOR THE FISH:
Canola oil for frying
3 tablespoons coriander seeds, toasted
    and ground (page 12)
1½ teaspoons freshly ground black
    pepper
3 tablespoons minced fresh ginger
1½ to 2 pounds fresh tuna, cut into
    1-inch-wide logs
Toasted sesame seeds (page 12), for
    garnish

Make the vegetable slaw: Stir the ginger, vinegar, and sugar into the mayonnaise. At least 1 hour before serving (but not more than 3 hours), toss the vegetables with the dressing. Refrigerate until ready to serve.

   When ready to cook, make the batter: Place the flour and baking powder in a bowl and stir in the club soda until smooth. Sprinkle with salt and pepper, and fold in the egg whites.

Meanwhile, heat 1 to 1 ½ inches of oil in a deep, heavy pot until it ripples but does not smoke. Mix the coriander, pepper, and ginger together. Sprinkle the fish with salt, then roll in the spice mixture. Set aside.

Working in batches if needed to avoid crowding the pan, dip a log of tuna in the batter and quickly slip it into the oil. If you like rare tuna, fry until the crust is golden brown on all sides; if you prefer your fish medium-rare or medium, let the crust reach a darker brown. Drain on paper towels. For serving, slice each log with a serrated knife, fan out the slices on a serving plate, and add a scoop of vegetable slaw. Sprinkle with sesame seeds and serve.

Coriander-Crust Tuna with Ginger-Orange-Braised Oxtail

This dish is a huge favorite at AZ, though the idea of fish and meat together may seem strange to you at first. Cooking mild, delicate fish with a little bit of intense spiced meat is traditional in Asian kitchens but rather unusual in Western ones—except for favorites like jambalaya and paella that combine shellfish and spicy sausage. Fresh tuna is an excellent candidate for this treatment; the dazzling flavor and texture of the oxtail "salad" acts as a spark for the simple fish, and the tuna's crunchy coriander seed crust rounds out the contrasts.

I serve this with a juicy, peppery arugula salad and perhaps Basic Rice (page 10) or even Gingered Hash Browns (page 104).

FOR THE OXTAILS:
5 pounds oxtails, trimmed of excess fat
1/2 cup Chinese fermented black beans (page 1)
Freshly grated zest of 2 oranges
3 cloves garlic, minced
1/4 cup canola oil
1 cup *each* diced onions, carrots, and celery
1 cup *each* red wine, rice wine (page 7), and plum wine (page 6), or 3 cups red wine
2 cups lightly salted Chicken Stock (page 13) or canned broth

FOR THE TUNA:
1/2 cup coriander seeds, toasted and ground (page 12)
1/4 cup minced fresh ginger
1 1/2 to 2 pounds fresh tuna, cut into 2-inch-wide logs
Kosher salt and freshly ground black pepper
2 tablespoons canola oil
Cilantro sprigs and finely shredded scallions, for garnish

Cook the oxtails: Place the oxtails in a large ceramic or glass bowl or a sealable thick plastic bag. Combine the black beans, zest, garlic, and oil in a blender and puree until smooth. Rub the puree into the oxtails, cover, and refrigerate for at least 12 hours and up to 24 hours. Bring to room temperature before cooking.

Heat a heavy-bottomed soup pot until very hot. Working in 2 batches to avoid crowding the pot, brown the oxtails on all sides. As they are browned, transfer the oxtails to a deep roasting pan. When all the oxtails are browned, add the onions, carrots, and celery to the empty pot (don't clean it out) and cook, stirring, until browned and softened, 8 to 10 minutes. Add the wines and bring to a boil, scraping up the browned bits from the bottom of the pot with a wooden spoon. Boil for 10 minutes.

Preheat the oven to 300 degrees. Pour the wine mixture and the stock over the oxtails in the roasting pan. Cover tightly with aluminum foil and bake for 3 hours or longer, until the meat is very tender and falling off the bone.

Lift the oxtails out of the liquid and set aside to cool. Use a slotted spoon to remove the vegetables from the braising liquid and discard them. On top of the stove, simmer the braising liquid in the roasting pan until it is reduced by half. When the oxtails are cool enough to handle, remove the meat from the bones and shred it finely. Return the meat to the liquid in the pan or place it in a clean saucepan and pour the liquid over.

(*The recipe can be made in advance up to this point and kept refrigerated up to 4 days.*) When ready to serve, gently reheat over medium-low heat.

Cook the tuna: Combine the coriander and ginger on a plate. Season the tuna logs all over with salt and pepper, then roll in the coriander mixture. Heat the oil in a large skillet over high heat. Sear the tuna quickly on all 4 sides, until browned on the outside but still red in the center. Slice the logs 1/2 inch thick and divide among serving plates. Use a slotted spoon to place a mound of oxtail on each plate. Garnish with cilantro sprigs and shreds of scallion, and serve.

Curried Monkfish "Osso Buco" with Slow-Roasted Tomatoes and Cauliflower Couscous

I adore the texture of osso buco, the Italian veal shank dish that you cook for hours until the meat collapses into mouthfuls of pure flavor. I couldn't resist adapting the method into a fish stew and was pleasantly surprised to see that the fish falls apart into juicy chunks after just 15 minutes of braising. My sauce combines red wine and lots of pungent spices that coat the fish with flavor, and the end result is still rich but much lighter and zingier than real osso buco.

I use the tail ends of whole monkfish, which are thick with a bone down the middle, like a shank. But monkfish steaks with a center bone will work just as well. If you prefer, you can gently simmer the dish on the stove instead of baking it in the oven.

4 tablespoons garam masala (page 4)
2 tablespoons java or another mild curry
   powder (page 3)
Kosher salt
4 to 6 (6- to 8-ounce) skinless monkfish
   "tails" or steaks (see note above)
¼ cup canola oil
1 onion, finely chopped
2 carrots, chopped
2 stalks celery, chopped
½ cup minced ginger
1 to 3 jalapeño chiles, minced
¼ cup minced garlic

2 cups chopped seeded fresh tomatoes or
   drained canned tomatoes
Freshly peeled zest of 2 lemons, cut into
   thin strips
2 cups red wine
2 cups lightly salted Chicken Stock
   (page 13), Shellfish Stock (page 15),
   or clam juice
Freshly ground black pepper
Cauliflower Couscous (recipe follows)
Slow-Roasted Tomatoes (recipe follows)
Whole cilantro leaves, for garnish

Mix the garam masala and curry powder together. Season the fish all over with salt, then generously dust all over with the spice mixture.

Heat the oven to 350 degrees. In a large, heavy pot with a lid (that can fit in your oven), heat the oil over high heat. Working in 2 batches if necessary to avoid crowding the pot, add the monkfish and sear on all sides until browned, adjusting the heat if necessary to prevent scorching. Remove the fish from the pan and set aside.

Add the onion, carrots, and celery to the hot pot and cook, stirring, until fragrant and softened, about 10 minutes. Add the ginger, jalapeños, and garlic, and cook, stirring, 5 minutes more. Add the tomatoes, zest, wine, and stock, and mix well. Bring to a boil. Return the monkfish to the pot, cover, and transfer to the hot oven. Bake for 15 minutes.

Remove the monkfish from the pot carefully; it is cooked through and will be ready to fall off the bone. Set aside. Boil the vegetables and liquid in the pot until reduced by half. Puree the mixture with a hand blender or pass through a food mill to make a smooth sauce. Strain into a clean pan and season to taste with salt and pepper. *(The recipe can be made in advance up to this point and kept refrigerated up to 2 days. It tastes best if served the day after it is made.)*

To serve, gently reheat the monkfish in the sauce. When heated through, serve over couscous with roasted tomatoes, garnished with cilantro leaves.

Cauliflower Couscous

I like the slightly chewy texture of Israeli couscous, which is a much bigger grain than the regular kind—almost the size of a pea. Both the cauliflower and the couscous are browned in butter, giving them a nutty, toasty flavor that is perfect with the fresh green herbs that are tossed in at the end.

6 tablespoons unsalted butter
Florets of 1 head cauliflower
Kosher salt and freshly ground black
   pepper
2 cups Israeli couscous

3 cups lightly salted Chicken Stock (page
   13), Shellfish Stock (page 15), or
   canned broth
1/2 cup minced parsley
1/2 cup minced fresh mint

Heat 3 tablespoons butter in a large skillet over high heat. When the butter is melted and just beginning to brown, add the cauliflower and cook, stirring, until soft and browned. Season to taste with salt and pepper, and set aside.

In a heavy saucepan with a lid, melt the remaining 3 tablespoons butter. Add

the couscous and toast, stirring constantly, until the grains are evenly coated and golden brown, about 5 minutes. Add 1 cup stock and bring to a rolling boil. Let cook until almost dry, then add another ½ cup stock. Repeat until the couscous is cooked through, using boiling water if you run out of stock, about 10 to 15 minutes. Set aside, covered, until ready to serve. When ready to serve, fluff the couscous with a fork and mix in the cauliflower, parsley, and mint. Season to taste with salt and pepper, and serve.

Slow-Roasted Tomatoes

MAKES
6 TO 8
SERVINGS

Somewhere between a vegetable and a condiment, these meaty tomato halves are the definition of savory. The slow roasting intensifies both the tanginess and the sweetness of the tomatoes. Serve them as a side dish for any fish or roast lamb, or as a snack on crusty bread with Parmesan cheese and a drizzle of olive oil.

15 plum tomatoes, cored and halved
  lengthwise
5 cloves garlic, minced
2 shallots, minced

2 tablespoons minced fresh thyme leaves
1 cup extra-virgin olive oil
Kosher salt and freshly ground black
  pepper

Heat the oven to 250 degrees. Squeeze the tomato halves to remove the seeds and arrange them in a roasting pan with the cut sides facing up. Mix the garlic, shallots, thyme, and oil together and drizzle over the tomatoes, making sure to fill up the empty seed cavities. Season generously with salt and pepper. Roast for 2 hours or longer, until very soft. Serve warm or at room temperature.

Seared Scallops with Wasabi Cucumber Salad and Port Glaze

Look no further—here is the perfect entrée for your next dinner party. Truly easy and wildly elegant, these crisp-crusted scallops glazed with a complex, tangy-sweet wine sauce take just 10 minutes to cook. When cooked over very high heat, scallops take on a wonderful mahogany crust and stay tender and juicy inside. The simple glaze can be simmered together up to a week in advance.

Apart from the cool cucumber salad, I'd serve this with nothing more than perfectly cooked basmati or jasmine rice.

FOR THE GLAZE:
2 cups ruby port
1 cup dry red wine
1 cup red wine vinegar
½ cup dark brown sugar
2 bay leaves

TO FINISH THE DISH:
16 to 20 large sea scallops, well drained
Kosher salt and freshly ground black
    pepper
2 tablespoons canola oil
Basic Rice (page 10; optional)
Wasabi Cucumber Salad (recipe follows)
Cilantro sprigs and finely shredded
    scallions, for garnish

Make the glaze: Combine all the ingredients in a saucepan, bring to a boil, and boil until reduced by three-fourths to about 1 cup, approximately 45 minutes. *(The glaze can be made in advance and kept refrigerated indefinitely.)*

When ready to cook, dry the scallops very well and sprinkle with salt and pepper. Heat a large, heavy skillet (preferably cast iron) and add the oil. Working in 2 batches if necessary, add the scallops and lower the heat to medium-high. Let the scallops cook undisturbed (resist the temptation to peek underneath or lift them off the pan) for about 4 minutes; they will take on a mahogany crust and will come away from the pan on their own. Add the glaze and let simmer for 2 minutes. Turn the scallops over and cook 1 minute more. Serve immediately over rice, if you like, with cucumber salad. Garnish with cilantro sprigs and shreds of scallion.

WASABI CUCUMBER SALAD

The best contrast for a sweet, tart dish like the one above is something cool, creamy, and peppery. This combination of cucumber and crème fraîche spiked with wasabi (Japanese horseradish powder) is perfect. The cream mellows out the fiery wasabi. Just don't mix the ingredients together until the last minute because the wasabi gets stronger as it sits. I love this salad as a side dish for fried fish or chicken—anything hot, crisp, and spicy.

1 hothouse (long seedless) cucumber, peeled
Salt
¼ cup minced chives
2 tablespoons crème fraîche

Freshly squeezed juice of 1 lemon
1 to 2 teaspoons wasabi (Japanese horseradish) powder (see Sources, page 233)

Cut the cucumber in half lengthwise and scrape out the seeds. Slice crosswise into very thin half-moons. Sprinkle the slices with salt and let sit for 15 minutes, then wrap them in a thin kitchen towel and gently wring out any excess water. Transfer to a bowl. Just before serving, drain off any additional liquid and fold in the remaining ingredients. Taste for salt and wasabi, and serve immediately.

Stir-Fried Egg Noodles with Shrimp and Shiitake Mushrooms

MAKES
4 SERVINGS

My favorite meal-in-a-bowl. I love this simple combination of tender noodles with shrimp, mushrooms, and snow peas, and it's also incredibly easy to toss together. If you like to order lo mein in Chinese restaurants, all the fresh flavor and great texture here will be a pleasant surprise—the dish is light, savory, and juicy. Feel free to put together any combination of "goodies" to toss with your noodles; this sauce is incredibly versatile. I let the heat of the wok thicken it instead of adding the usual cornstarch.

FOR THE SAUCE:
¼ cup soy sauce
¼ cup water
2 tablespoons hoisin sauce (page 4)
1 tablespoon sesame oil
1 teaspoon fish sauce (page 3)
1 jalapeño chile, minced
2 tablespoons minced fresh ginger
2 cloves garlic, minced

FOR THE STIR-FRY:
12 ounces dried thin egg noodles
2 teaspoons Scallion Oil (page 12) or canola oil
3 tablespoons canola oil
16 large shrimp, peeled and deveined
16 small shiitake mushroom caps, quartered
½ cup oyster mushrooms, sliced
2 cups soybean sprouts (page 61) or thinly sliced asparagus
½ cup sugar snap or snow pea pods, thinly sliced on the diagonal
Kosher salt and freshly ground black pepper
Cilantro sprigs and finely shredded scallions, for garnish

Make the sauce: Stir all the ingredients together and set aside.

Bring a large pot of unsalted water to a boil. Cook the noodles according to the instructions on the package. Drain, toss in Scallion Oil, and set aside.

When ready to cook, heat a large wok or deep skillet over high heat. Add the 3 tablespoons canola oil and swirl to coat. Heat the oil until it ripples. Add the shrimp and cook, tossing, for 3 to 4 minutes. In order, add the shiitakes, oyster mushrooms, bean sprouts, and peas, tossing after each addition. Add the noodles and pour in the sauce. Cook, tossing, until the vegetables are just cooked through and everything is evenly coated with the sauce. Add salt and pepper to taste. Serve in a large bowl, garnished with cilantro sprigs and shreds of scallion.

SAMBAL-GRILLED SHRIMP WITH MINTED SOYBEAN WONTONS AND TOMATO WATER

MAKES
4 TO 6
SERVINGS

Most of my culinary influences are Asian and American, but there are also a few echoes of the years I spent at an English boarding school—cooking peas with fresh mint is one. English cooks treat their sweet, fresh peas with a great deal of respect, and season them as lightly as possible. I apply that delicate touch to edamame, the fresh green soybeans that remind me of peas, creating a fragrant filling for wontons that contrasts wonderfully with spicy, bold grilled shrimp. The dish swims in a savory, tart "tomato water" that pulls all the flavors together.

Finally, a tangle of pea shoots on top boosts the pea flavor. The combination of peas, mint, shrimp, and tomatoes is one that everyone seems to love.

FOR THE WONTONS:
1 cup shelled edamame (soybeans),
   fresh or frozen
1 tablespoon sugar
¼ cup minced mint leaves
¼ cup canola oil
¼ cup lightly salted Chicken Stock
   (page 13) or water
Salt
24 round yellow wonton wrappers (also
   called Hong Kong–style wrappers)

TO FINISH THE DISH:
24 large shrimp, peeled and deveined
4 cloves garlic, chopped
2 tablespoons *sambal* (page 8)
¼ cup canola oil
1 cup thinly sliced sugar snap or
   snow pea pods
1 cup pea shoots or baby salad greens
¼ cup Soy-Lime Vinaigrette (page 59)
2 cups Tomato Water (recipe follows)

Make the wontons: Bring a saucepan of water and a pinch of sugar (to help set the green color) to a boil. Add the soybeans and boil for 3 to 5 minutes. Drain well and transfer to a food processor. (If using frozen soybeans, blanch them according to the directions on the package and shell them afterward; place the shelled beans in the food processor.)

Add the sugar, mint, oil, and stock. Pulse the mixture until almost smooth, adding a little more stock or oil as needed to make the filling silky. Season to taste with salt.

Lay a wrapper on a work surface. Place a teaspoon of filling in the center and brush a little water around the edges of the wrapper. Lift one edge of the wrapper over the filling and press it to the opposite edge, making a half-moon. Press the edges together to seal. Brush a little more water on the 2 corners and lift the wonton up by the corners. Gently lift the round part of the half-moon up and over the straight edge (this will make a twist at each corner). Then bring the 2 corners together and press gently to seal, making a shape rather like tortellini. Set aside and repeat. *(The recipe can be made in advance up to this point and kept refrigerated, lightly covered with a clean towel, up to 1 day.)*

When ready to serve, cook the wontons: Bring a large pot of salted water to a boil. Gently add the wontons and boil until they rise to the top, which means that they are cooked through. Lift out with a slotted spoon and reserve.

Cook the shrimp: Rinse them well and pat dry. Toss them in a bowl with the garlic, *sambal*, and oil. Let marinate up to 30 minutes. Heat a grill until medium-hot. Add the shrimp and grill about 3 minutes on each side, just until cooked through. (Or sear the marinated shrimp on both sides in a heavy skillet. Lift the shrimp out of the skillet and pour in the tomato water, stirring to heat it through and season it.)

To serve, toss the pea pods and pea shoots with the vinaigrette. Place 4 wontons in each serving bowl, interspersing them with grilled shrimp. Pour about 1/3 cup of warm tomato water into each bowl. Top with a little mound of pea salad and serve.

Tomato Water

The perfect tomato, in liquid form. You'll be amazed at the powerful tomato flavor that is packed into a spoonful of this pale liquid, produced by slowly separating the tomato essence from the actual tomato. The result is sweet, salty, and tart, like a light but complex broth or sauce. It makes a wonderful base for light vegetable soups or as a refreshing cold consommé served in thin teacups.

MAKES
ABOUT
2 CUPS

5 large, ripe tomatoes, cored   1 tablespoon kosher salt

In a food processor, puree the tomatoes with the salt. Line a fine strainer with cheesecloth and place over a bowl to hold the liquid. Pour the tomato puree into the lined strainer and set aside for at least 8 hours or overnight. The "water" that collects will be clear to pale yellow. Gently heat just before serving.

THAI *BOUILLABAISSE* WITH BLACKFISH, MUSSELS, CLAMS, AND SPINACH

MAKES
4 SERVINGS

I have long been addicted to the aromatic broths of Southeast Asia. Red with chile, green with herbs, and scented with lemongrass, they are eaten every day in endless variations in Malaysia, Thailand, and Singapore. This steamy, highly perfumed brew is my marriage of tom yum, *the classic Thai soup with shrimp and mushrooms, and* French bouillabaisse. *In both dishes the method of poaching fish in the spiced broth leaves it flaky, white, and juicy. I'm fond of the Asian habit of stirring fresh greens into simmering soups, so I add spinach at the last minute.*

FOR THE BROTH:
4 cups lightly salted Shellfish Stock (page 15), Chicken Stock (page 13), canned broth, or clam juice
2 red onions, sliced
1 green apple, peeled and roughly chopped
1 stalk lemongrass, tough ends trimmed off and discarded, smashed in a few places with the handle of a knife
½ cup thickly sliced fresh ginger (no need to peel it)
2 jalapeño chiles, roughly chopped
2 Thai bird chiles (page 2)
4 kaffir lime leaves (page 4) or 4 teaspoons freshly grated lime zest
2 cups cilantro leaves
2 cups mint leaves
2 cups basil leaves

2 tablespoons fish sauce (page 3), or more to taste
2 tablespoons freshly squeezed lime juice, or more to taste
Kosher salt and freshly ground black pepper

TO FINISH THE DISH:
4 (4- to 5-ounce) pieces blackfish, halibut, or cod
12 mussels
12 small clams, such as Manila, or cockles
2 cups spinach leaves
Cooked rice or noodles or Thai Rice Noodle Salad (page 118), for serving
Cilantro sprigs and finely shredded scallions, for garnish

Make the broth: Combine the stock, onions, apple, lemongrass, ginger, both chiles, and lime leaves in a large pot and bring to a boil. Lower the heat to a simmer and simmer for 15 minutes. Turn off the heat and add the cilantro, mint, and basil.

Infuse for 15 minutes. Strain the broth into a clean saucepan. Season to taste with fish sauce, lime juice, salt, and pepper. *(The broth can be made in advance up to this point and kept refrigerated up to 2 days.)*

When ready to serve, heat the broth to a simmer over high heat. Add the fish, mussels, and clams, and cover. Cook for 5 minutes, or until the mussels and clams open. Stir in the spinach just until it wilts. In each bowl, pour broth over rice or noodles, place the shellfish on top, and garnish with cilantro and scallion.

Spicy Coconut Soup with Shellfish, Fresh Herbs, and Noodles

A dish that snaps me right back to childhood days in Malaysia is laksa, *a simple but heady brew of coconut milk, stock, and aromatics such as shallots and lemongrass. It's classic Kuala Lumpur street food but also nourishing, comforting home cooking. My grandmother made a big pot of* laksa *each morning, and we'd eat it throughout the day, slurping it with noodles for lunch and adding grilled shellfish for dinner. The fresh noodle salad studded with herbs in this recipe makes the dish my own.*

Dried shrimp, like anchovy paste, brings out the flavors of ingredients without being assertive on its own. The shrimp will smell extremely strong at first, but cooking really tames them.

FOR THE BROTH:

¼ cup dried shrimp, soaked and drained (page 8)
2 large cloves garlic, peeled
2 tablespoons chopped fresh ginger
1 jalapeño chile, stemmed
1 tablespoon canola oil
5 shallots, thinly sliced
1½ teaspoons red curry paste (page 3)
1½ teaspoons java curry powder (page 3) or another curry powder of your choice
1 cup dry vermouth
1 (14-ounce) can coconut milk
2 cups clam juice
Salt
1 kaffir lime leaf (page 4) *or* 1 teaspoon lime zest
½ lemongrass stalk, tough ends trimmed off and discarded

TO FINISH THE DISH:

1 pound rice vermicelli (page 7)
¼ cup Scallion Oil (page 12) *or* canola oil mixed with 1 tablespoon minced scallions
½ cup shredded fresh mint
½ cup shredded cilantro
1 mango, peeled, seeded, and finely diced
½ cup matchstick-size pieces of daikon or watermelon radish
16 to 20 mussels in the shell, well rinsed
16 to 20 littleneck clams in the shell, well rinsed
Cilantro sprigs and finely shredded scallions, for garnish

Make the broth: Combine the shrimp, garlic, ginger, and chile in a food processor and pulse together until finely chopped. In a medium soup pot, heat the oil over medium-high heat. Add the shrimp mixture and cook, stirring, until very fragrant, golden, and just beginning to brown. Add the shallots, curry paste, and curry powder, and cook, stirring occasionally, until the shallots are soft. Add the vermouth and bring to a boil, stirring to scrape up the browned bits from the bottom of the pan. Simmer until the liquid is reduced by half. Add the coconut milk and clam juice, simmer for 10 minutes, then remove from the heat. Season to taste with salt. Strain into a clean pot, add the lime leaf (if using lime zest, do not add at this time) and lemongrass, and set aside to infuse while you prepare the other ingredients. After about 30 minutes, remove the lime leaf and lemongrass.

Rehydrate the rice noodles: Bring a medium-size pot of water to a rolling boil, then turn off the heat and immediately add the noodles. Let soak for 2 to 3 minutes, moving the noodles around in the water to separate the strands. When soft, drain well and toss with the Scallion Oil.

When ready to serve, add the mint, cilantro, mango, and radish to the noodles and toss well. Bring the coconut broth to a boil and add the mussels and clams, simmering them until they open. While the shellfish cook, divide the noodles among serving bowls. (If using lime zest, add it to the broth at this time.) Spoon the broth around the noodles and divide the shellfish on top, discarding any that do not open. Serve immediately, sprinkled with cilantro sprigs and shreds of scallion.

Chicken and Duck Main Courses

CHICKEN AND BLACK MUSHROOM DUMPLINGS IN AROMATIC DOUBLE-CHICKEN BROTH

FESTIVE ROAST CHICKEN WITH RICE AND MUSHROOM STUFFING

BONELESS CHICKEN *DHANSAK* WITH LENTILS AND PISTACHIO–GOLDEN RAISIN PILAF

GOANESE COCONUT CHICKEN CURRY WITH *PURI* BREAD

CHINESE ONE-POT CHICKEN AND RICE

GRILLED FIVE-SPICE CHICKEN

AROMATIC RED-COOKED CHICKEN WITH BLACK MUSHROOMS, GARLIC, AND *KAI LAN*

LAPSANG SOUCHONG–MARINATED CHICKEN WITH FIG CHUTNEY AND SCALLION PANCAKES

ORANGE *MU SHU* DUCK WITH CRANBERRY WILD RICE AND BRANDIED HOISIN SAUCE

CRISPY DUCK SCHNITZEL WITH HAZELNUT BROWN BUTTER AND BEET, ORANGE, AND ARUGULA SALAD

CRISPED DUCK BREAST WITH LEMONGRASS GLAZE AND SWEET POTATO–COCONUT PUREE

CHICKEN AND BLACK MUSHROOM DUMPLINGS IN AROMATIC DOUBLE-CHICKEN BROTH

I am a big fan of chicken soup, especially when it's full of what I think of as "goodies." I'm always happy with a bowl of matzo ball or wonton or chicken noodle soup, no matter where in the world it comes from. To make the soup really satisfying, the broth itself has to have good flavor, so I like to make double-chicken broth. Instead of adding plain water to the chicken bones to simmer into stock, you add a mild chicken broth and ginger, cilantro, and scallions for flavor. It's fine to start with canned broth, since you'll be punching up its flavor with many fresh aromatics.

The juicy, peppery wontons make this a hearty entrée. You can also add cooked egg noodles along with (or even instead of) the wontons.

FOR THE BROTH:
3 to 4 quarts lightly salted Chicken Stock (page 13)
1 (2-pound) chicken *or* 2 pounds whole chicken legs and thighs
1/2 cup thickly sliced fresh ginger (no need to peel it)
1 bunch cilantro, including stems
1 bunch scallions, white ends smashed

FOR THE WONTONS:
1 cup ground dark meat chicken
1/4 cup ground pork or additional ground chicken
1/4 cup diced dried black mushrooms, soaked (page 6), or fresh shiitake mushrooms
1/4 cup finely diced celery
2 tablespoons chopped garlic chives or plain chives

1/4 cup fish sauce (page 3)
1/4 teaspoon kosher salt
1/4 teaspoon finely ground white pepper
About 1 tablespoon white wine
25 round wonton wrappers

TO FINISH THE SOUP:
1 cup carrots, cut into 1/4-inch dice
1 cup shiitake mushroom caps, sliced 1/4 inch thick
1 cup shredded Napa cabbage
1 cup spinach, Chinese broccoli, or baby bok choy
1 cup firm tofu, cut into 1/2-inch dice
Fish sauce (page 3)
Soy sauce
Cilantro sprigs and finely shredded scallions, for garnish

In a large pot, combine the stock and chicken. Bring to a simmer (do not let it reach a boil) and simmer, uncovered, for 35 minutes. Add the ginger, cilantro, and scallions, and simmer 10 minutes more. Turn off the heat and let infuse for an additional 15 minutes. Strain into another large pot. Shred the meat from the chicken and reserve.

Make the wontons: Combine the chicken, pork, mushrooms, celery, chives, fish sauce, salt, and pepper in a bowl. Sprinkle in a little white wine to help the mixture hold together. (If you like, at this point you can fry a little cake of the mixture to taste for seasoning.) Wrap a scant tablespoon of the mixture in each wonton wrapper: Place the filling in the center of the wrapper and gather the edges of the wrapper together on top like a beggar's purse. Twist and pinch the top with wet fingers to seal it closed. Set aside under a slightly damp towel.

Bring the broth to a rolling boil. Add the carrots, mushrooms, cabbage, and spinach, lower the heat to a simmer, and simmer for 5 minutes. Add the wontons and reserved chicken meat, and simmer 10 minutes more. Just before serving, stir in the tofu and season to taste with fish sauce and soy sauce. Garnish with cilantro sprigs and shreds of scallion, and serve in large, deep bowls.

FESTIVE ROAST CHICKEN WITH RICE AND MUSHROOM STUFFING

My family always celebrates Thanksgiving by stuffing a turkey with this aromatic rice mixture, but I love it so much that I use the recipe year-round for roast chicken. It's all the yummy little bits sprinkled in the stuffing that keep me coming back: shallots, sausage, celery, mushrooms, and chestnuts. The sticky rice becomes dense and fully flavored as it cooks inside the bird, just like bread stuffing. This recipe makes more stuffing than you need for one bird. You can bake the extra to serve alongside, or use the recipe to stuff two smaller chickens.

After the final touch of a gingery glaze, painted on at the end, the finished bird is brown and glossy, with slightly crisped skin. For a festive dinner, serve it with Braised Broccoli Rabe (page 194) and Sweet Potato–Coconut Puree (page 171).

FOR THE STUFFING:
2 tablespoons canola oil
¼ cup finely diced Chinese sausage (page 8)
½ cup finely diced pancetta (uncured bacon) or regular bacon
½ cup chopped shallots
½ cup chopped celery
2 tablespoons dried shrimp, soaked and drained (page 8)
1 cup shiitake mushroom caps, diced
½ cup roasted and peeled whole chestnuts (optional)
2 cups cooked Sticky Rice or Basic Rice (page 10)
½ cup lightly salted Chicken Stock (page 13) or canned broth
Kosher salt and freshly ground black pepper

FOR THE CHICKEN:
1 (4-pound) chicken, giblets removed, extra fat trimmed off
1 cup *each* diced onions, celery, and carrots
¼ cup soy sauce
2 tablespoons minced fresh ginger
2 tablespoons Cognac or another brandy
1 cup white wine
Cilantro sprigs and finely shredded scallions, for garnish

Heat the canola oil in a large skillet over high heat. Add the sausage and pancetta, lower the heat to medium, and slowly brown the meat, stirring occasionally. Remove the meat with a slotted spoon and set aside. Add the shallots and celery to the fat in the pan, raise the heat to medium-high, and cook, stirring, until softened and translucent, about 10 minutes. Add the shrimp and shiitakes. Cook, stirring, until fragrant. Return the meat to the pan and add the chestnuts, rice, and stock. Cook, stirring, until the mixture is heated through and the stock has been absorbed. Set aside to cool. Season to taste with salt and pepper.

Heat the oven to 400 degrees. Rinse and dry the chicken and season it inside and out with salt and pepper. Stuff the rice mixture into the cavity and truss the chicken (or, if you don't truss the whole chicken, at least sew the cavity closed). Mix the onion, celery, and carrots in the bottom of a roasting pan. Place the chicken breast side up on the vegetables and roast for 30 minutes. Lower the heat to 325 and roast 30 minutes more.

Meanwhile, mix the soy sauce, ginger, and brandy in a bowl. As the chicken roasts, baste it with the glaze every 10 to 15 minutes.

Check the chicken for doneness by sticking the tip of a knife into the joint where the thigh meets the body; the juices should run clear, with no trace of pink. Lift out of the pan and set aside to rest for 10 minutes before removing the stuffing and carving the bird. Meanwhile, make the sauce: Pour the wine into the roasting pan with the vegetables and set over medium heat. Simmer for 7 to 10 minutes, then strain into a serving pitcher or gravy boat. Taste for salt and pepper.

Garnish the dish with cilantro sprigs and shreds of scallion, and serve.

Boneless Chicken *Dhansak* with Lentils and Pistachio–Golden Raisin Pilaf

MAKES
4 TO 6
SERVINGS

Curries and dals, or lentils, are a classic combination at the Indian table. In this recipe, the curry and dal are brewed together into a delicious stew; the lentils and other vegetables provide a thick, lusciously spiced sauce for the chicken. Tomatoes, lime juice, garlic, and ginger brighten up the flavors.

This one-pot dish can also be made very successfully with lamb or beef instead of chicken. Serve it with nothing more than basmati rice and a green salad.

3 cardamom pods, crushed and seeds removed (discard the outer husks)
¼ teaspoon whole cloves
2 star anise pods
¼ teaspoon fenugreek seeds
1 tablespoon Aleppo chile pepper (page 1)
1½ teaspoons black peppercorns
1 teaspoon white peppercorns
1 cup yellow lentils (page 5)
2½ cups water
½ cup chopped cilantro
2 large onions, chopped
1 cup butternut or kabocha squash, cut into 1-inch dice
2 boiling potatoes, cut into ¾-inch dice
¼ cup canola oil

4 large boneless, skinless chicken breast halves, cut into 1-inch dice
1 (2-inch) piece fresh ginger, peeled and minced
6 cloves garlic, minced
1 to 2 jalapeño chiles, seeded and minced
2 teaspoons tomato paste
1 tablespoon palm sugar (page 8) or dark brown sugar
1 teaspoon wine vinegar
1½ cups lightly salted Chicken Stock (page 13) or canned broth, or water
Freshly squeezed juice of 1 to 2 limes
Kosher salt and freshly ground black pepper
Pistachio–Golden Raisin Pilaf (recipe follows)

Heat a large, heavy skillet over high heat. Lower the heat to medium and add the cardamom, cloves, star anise, fenugreek, chile pepper, and both peppercorns, and toast, stirring, until the spices are darkened and fragrant, about 3 minutes. Transfer to a plate to cool, then grind in a spice grinder until fine but not powdery.

In a large pot, combine the lentils, water, cilantro, onions, squash, potatoes, and

2 teaspoons of spice mixture. Bring to a boil, lower to a simmer, and simmer, stirring often and adding water if the mixture seems to be getting too dry, until the lentils and vegetables are very soft. Set aside to cool, then puree with a hand blender or in a food processor (or simply mix vigorously, breaking up the lentils and vegetables with a sturdy whisk).

Heat the oil in another large pot over high heat. Add the chicken pieces and the remaining spices, and cook, stirring to brown on all sides. Lower the heat to avoid scorching. Add the ginger, garlic, and jalapeño, and cook, stirring, just until softened. Pour in the lentil puree. Add the tomato paste, sugar, vinegar, and stock, and bring to a boil. Lower the heat to a simmer, cover, and simmer for 30 minutes. Add the lime juice, salt, and pepper to taste. (*The recipe can be made in advance and kept refrigerated up to 4 days.*)

Just before serving, taste for lime juice. Serve on a bed of pilaf, garnished with cilantro.

Pistachio-Golden Raisin Pilaf

This is my own favorite pilaf, studded with nuts and raisins and scented with spice. In a break with Indian tradition, I like to remove the whole spices after the cooking, so I tie them up in cheesecloth at the beginning of the recipe. Then it's easy to just pull out the spices and toss them away at the end.

1 (3-inch) cinnamon stick
6 cardamom pods, lightly crushed
10 black peppercorns
½ teaspoon fennel seeds
1 tablespoon clarified butter (page 2) or
    a combination of vegetable oil and
    butter
1 onion, chopped

2 cups basmati rice
2½ cups water
½ cup lightly salted Chicken Stock
    (page 13) or canned broth or water
½ teaspoon salt
¼ cup golden raisins
½ cup chopped pistachio nuts

Wrap the cinnamon stick, cardamom pods, peppercorns, and fennel seeds in a piece of cheesecloth. Tie tightly with string.

Heat the butter in a heavy pot (with a tight-fitting lid) over medium-high heat. Add the onion and cook, stirring often, until the edges are golden brown. Add the rice and toast, stirring constantly to lightly coat each grain of rice with butter. Add the water, stock, spice bag, and salt, and bring to a boil. Cover, lower the heat, and simmer undisturbed for 15 minutes. Turn off the heat and sprinkle the raisins and pistachios on top of the rice. Replace the cover on the pot and let sit undisturbed for 10 minutes. Use chopsticks or a large fork to fluff the rice and mix in the raisins and pistachios. Remove and discard the spice bag. Keep covered until ready to serve; the rice will stay hot for at least 30 minutes.

Goanese Coconut Chicken Curry with *Puri* Bread

MAKES
4 SERVINGS

My mother has many friends in the Indian community within Kuala Lumpur, and she often trades recipes with them. This rich, savory chicken curry is called shakuti *in Goa, the coastal region of southwest India it hails from. The fish sauce and lemon juice are probably Malaysian additions to the original dish.*

Like many Indian recipes, this one begins with a super-slow caramelizing of chopped onions. When cooked until soft and dark golden, the onions melt into the sauce, leaving only their deep flavor behind.

3 Thai bird chiles (page 2), stemmed and
 seeded
2 tablespoons cumin seeds
1 teaspoon coriander seeds
1 teaspoon fenugreek seeds
½ teaspoon black peppercorns
½ teaspoon cloves
4 cardamom pods, crushed and seeds
 removed (discard the outer husks)
1 (3-inch) cinnamon stick, broken into
 pieces
1 teaspoon turmeric
3 tablespoons canola oil
2 onions, chopped

3 cloves garlic, minced
½ cup unsweetened shredded coconut
1 (4-pound) chicken, cut into 8 serving
 pieces
¼ cup chopped roasted peanuts
 (page 11)
½ cup coconut milk
½ cup lightly salted Chicken Stock
 (page 13) or canned broth or water
Freshly squeezed juice of 2 lemons
Fish sauce (page 3)
Cilantro leaves, for garnish
Puri Bread (recipe follows) or
 Basic Rice (page 10), for serving

Heat a large heavy skillet over high heat. Lower the heat to medium and add the chiles, cumin, coriander, fenugreek, peppercorns, and cloves, and toast, stirring, until the spices are darkened and fragrant, about 3 minutes. Transfer to a plate to cool, then transfer to a spice grinder and add the cardamom and cinnamon. Grind until fine but not powdery. Mix in the turmeric.

In a large, heavy pot, heat the oil over high heat and add the onions. Cook, stirring often, until the onions are well caramelized, meltingly soft, and dark golden brown; this may take up to 30 minutes. Adjust the heat to prevent scorching. When the onions are about 5 minutes away from being fully cooked, add the garlic.

Raise the heat and add the spices and coconut. Let sizzle for about 1 minute, stirring constantly. Push the spice-onion mixture aside and add the chicken to the pot. Brown the chicken lightly on all sides. Add the peanuts, coconut milk, and stock, bring to a simmer, and simmer, uncovered, for 30 minutes. Stir in the lemon juice and fish sauce, and simmer 15 minutes more. Taste for salt. Sprinkle with cilantro and serve with plenty of *puri* or rice to sop up the delicious sauce.

Puri (Indian Balloon) Bread

MAKES 12

Puri is the lightest bread in the Indian kitchen. It puffs up like a balloon when fried, then collapses into a flaky flatbread that's wonderful for soaking up sauces. If it's going to be eaten on its own or with a simple lentil soup, I like to season it lightly with spices or dried chile powder.

2 cups all-purpose flour
1/2 teaspoon salt
2 tablespoons clarified butter
  (page 2)

1/2 cup warm water
2 tablespoons peanut oil, plus extra for
  frying

Sift the flour and salt into the bowl of a mixer fitted with a dough hook or a food processor fitted with a plastic blade. Mix in the clarified butter, water, and 2 tablespoons peanut oil to make a rough dough. Knead or process until the dough is soft and elastic, about 10 minutes. Cover the dough and let rest at room temperature for 1 hour. Knead the dough lightly and divide into 12 reasonably equal balls. Roll out each ball into a circle about 5 inches across.

Place a brown paper bag or a sheet pan lined with paper towels by the stove. Heat 1 1/2 inches of peanut oil in a deep skillet over high heat until it ripples. Lower the heat to medium and add a dough round to the oil. It will sink to the bottom of the pot, then rise to the top and start to puff up. Let cook until golden brown on the bottom, about 1 ½ minutes, then turn with tongs and cook 1 minute more. Adjust the heat to keep the oil bubbling briskly around the puri. Lift out and let drain. Repeat with the remaining dough rounds. Serve as soon as possible.

CHINESE ONE-POT CHICKEN AND RICE

Here's China's entry in the worldwide pageant of delicious chicken and rice dishes. Like paella, jambalaya, *and* arroz con pollo, *this savory, homey dish cooks all in one pot; in fact, my grandmother and aunts used to make it right in the electric rice cooker (but a big heavy pot works fine). The results are always fragrant, flavorful, and somehow comforting to eat.*

Each bite is packed with flavorful bits of mushrooms, shallots, Chinese sausage, and fresh ginger. When you drizzle on the sesame oil before serving, the heat releases all of its nutty depth.

2 tablespoons white wine
1/2 teaspoon cornstarch
1 egg white
2 boneless chicken breast halves or
    4 boneless chicken thighs, sliced across
    the grain into 1/2-inch-thick strips
1/4 cup canola oil
1/4 cup thinly sliced shallots
2 tablespoons fresh ginger, cut into thin
    matchsticks
2 cups long-grain rice
2 Chinese sausages (page 8),
    thinly sliced

8 dried black mushrooms, soaked (page 6;
    reserve 1 cup soaking liquid) and thinly
    sliced, or fresh shiitake mushroom caps,
    thinly sliced
3 cups lightly salted Chicken Stock
    (page 13; 4 cups if you are using
    fresh mushrooms) or canned broth
Kosher salt and freshly ground black
    pepper
1 teaspoon dark sesame oil
2 teaspoons soy sauce
Cilantro sprigs and finely shredded
    scallions, for garnish

Whisk the white wine and cornstarch together. In a large bowl, lightly whisk the egg white. Whisk in the cornstarch mixture. Add the chicken and toss until well coated. Set aside.

Heat the oil in a large skillet over medium-high heat. Add the shallots and cook, stirring often, until golden, about 10 minutes. Add the ginger and cook 1 minute more. Add the rice and cook, stirring, until toasted and golden.

Meanwhile, heat the oven to 400 degrees. Scrape the rice mixture into a soaked clay pot or a heavy casserole with a tight-fitting lid. Fold in the chicken, sausages, and mushrooms. Pour in the stock and reserved mushroom soaking liquid (or all stock), cover, and bake for 30 minutes, or until the rice is cooked. The casserole will stay hot for at least 30 minutes after you remove it from the oven.

Just before serving, gently stir the casserole and add salt and pepper to taste. Drizzle with sesame oil and soy sauce, and sprinkle with cilantro sprigs and shreds of scallion.

GRILLED FIVE-SPICE CHICKEN

MAKES
4 SERVINGS

This recipe always takes me back to one of my favorite restaurants in San Francisco, a little family-run storefront that served just one dish: perfect grilled chicken. The Vietnamese family that ran the place had truly mastered the flavorings and the method, and the result was irresistible. With the chicken you get a choice of rice or noodles plus a salad, and that's exactly what I serve with my version. It's an ideal weeknight dinner.

You can also broil the chicken or cook it in a heavy grill pan.

1 (3½- to 4-pound) chicken, cut into
   8 pieces
2 cloves garlic, minced
¼ cup rice wine vinegar
2 tablespoons sugar
2 tablespoons soy sauce

1 teaspoon dark sesame oil
¼ cup dark brown sugar
1 tablespoon five-spice powder
   (page 4)
Cilantro sprigs and finely shredded
   scallions, for garnish

Rinse the chicken and pat dry. Mix the remaining ingredients together (except the cilantro and scallions) in a container large enough to hold the chicken pieces. Add the chicken, turn to coat, and marinate at least 2 hours or up to 8 hours. Drain.

Preheat a grill to medium-high. Place the chicken on the grill, skin side down, and grill without moving for 10 minutes, until the skin is brown and crispy. Turn and grill until cooked through, 10 to 15 minutes more. Garnish with cilantro sprigs and shreds of scallion, and serve.

Aromatic Red-Cooked Chicken with Black Mushrooms, Garlic, and *Kai Lan*

FALL/WINTER

This is the spot where Chinese home cooking and French home cooking intersect: a savory chicken stew packed with mushrooms, garlic, shallots, and greens, a perfect one-pot meal with rice or noodles. To braise the chicken I've combined my grand-mother's red cooking method (a traditional combination of soy sauce and caramel; she and many other Chinese cooks use Coca-Cola for the caramel these days) and French coq au vin, where the chicken is steeped in red wine. The finished dish is saucy, deeply flavored, and supremely satisfying.

For extra richness in the sauce you might want to add 4 ounces of diced pork belly or pancetta to brown in the pot along with the shallots. Kai lan is Chinese broc-coli; broccoli rabe makes a good substitute. The kai lan in this recipe will cook down and become very tender. If you prefer bright green, crisp vegetables, blanch the broc-coli separately until just tender and stir it into the stew just before serving.

1 large (about 4 pounds) chicken, cut into 10 pieces (your butcher can do this for you)
10 diced dried black mushrooms, soaked in hot water until soft, or fresh shiitake mushroom caps
10 shallots, peeled and left whole
20 cloves garlic, peeled and left whole
1 cup red wine
1 cup lightly salted Chicken Stock (page 13) or canned broth

1 cup soy sauce
1 cup Coca-Cola
1 star anise pod
1 (3-inch) cinnamon stick
2 Thai bird chiles (page 2)
About 1½ pounds Chinese broccoli (*kai lan*) or broccoli rabe, cut into 1-inch lengths
Salt and freshly ground pepper
Basic Rice (page 10), for serving

Preheat the oven to 350 degrees.

Heat a large, heavy ovenproof casserole over high heat. Working with 2 batches if necessary to avoid crowding the pan, brown the chicken well on both sides, removing each piece as it is cooked. When all the chicken is browned and the pan is empty, add the mushrooms and shallots to the drippings in the pan and cook, stirring, over high heat just until browned. Add the garlic and browned chicken.

Pour the red wine, stock, soy sauce, and Coca-Cola into the pot and bring to a boil. Lower the heat and simmer for 5 minutes. Add the star anise, cinnamon, and chiles. Stir in the *kai lan*, cover the pot tightly, and bake for 45 minutes. Before serving, check the sauce; if it is thin, uncover the pot and simmer to thicken. Add salt and pepper to taste and remove the spices and chiles. Serve with rice.

Lapsang Souchong–Marinated Chicken with Fig Chutney and Scallion Pancakes

This wonderful dish began life as classic Chinese Peking duck and evolved into golden, juicy, pan-roasted chicken served with fragrant, crisp scallion pancakes and a sweet, tangy chutney full of figs and spice to pull all the tastes together. You'll soon see why this never comes off the menu at AZ. It combines two of my favorite tricks, marinating and brining, to add smokiness, sweetness, depth, and juiciness to the chicken. Using a sweet juice like pineapple in your marinades really helps the chicken brown in the pan because the natural sugars caramelize quickly over high heat. Lapsang souchong tea adds its smoky flavor, and the natural acids in the tea act as tenderizers.

This recipe for scallion pancakes is my easy rendition of the Chinese classic street food. But you can serve plain rice tossed with a little fresh scallion instead if you prefer.

FOR THE MARINADE:
2 cups pineapple juice
1 cup kosher salt
1 cinnamon stick
2 star anise pods
1 onion, coarsely chopped
2 cloves
2 bay leaves
½ cup lapsang souchong tea leaves

TO FINISH THE DISH:
8 large chicken pieces, either breasts or whole legs, with the skin (boneless breasts are fine, too)
1 tablespoon canola oil
Cilantro sprigs and finely shredded scallions, for garnish
Fig Chutney (recipe follows)
Scallion Pancakes (recipe follows)

Make the marinade: In a large pot, bring all the ingredients to a boil over high heat. Lower the heat, simmer for 5 minutes, then cool to room temperature.

When cool, pour marinade over the chicken. Cover and refrigerate 4 to 8 hours.

Heat the oil in a large skillet (preferably cast iron) over high heat. When the oil is very hot, add the chicken, skin side down. (Cook in 2 batches if needed to avoid crowding.) Turn the heat to medium-high and let the chicken brown undisturbed for 5 minutes. Turn once and continue cooking 4 minutes more, or until cooked through. Sprinkle with cilantro and scallion. Serve with fig chutney and scallion pancakes.

Fig Chutney

The combination of dried and fresh figs in this chutney makes it really special, and it couldn't be easier to make. The sweetness is great with chicken and duck dishes.

1 tablespoon canola oil
½ onion, chopped
1 large Granny Smith apple, peeled and
   chopped
6 large dried figs, chopped
½ cup apple cider vinegar

½ cup plum wine or another sweet wine,
   such as Sauternes or tawny port
Kosher salt and freshly ground black
   pepper
6 large fresh figs, quartered

Heat the oil in a medium pot over high heat. Add the onion and apple, lower the heat to medium, and cook, stirring, until the onion is soft and translucent. Do not let it brown.

Add the dried figs, vinegar, and wine. Bring to a boil, lower the heat, and simmer for 10 minutes, or until the figs start to fall apart. Set aside at room temperature. Season to taste with salt and pepper. Just before serving, fold in the fresh figs.

Scallion Pancakes

1 ½ cups cake flour
¼ cup all-purpose flour
1 teaspoon salt
1 tablespoon plus ¾ cup canola oil

¾ cup boiling water
2 tablespoons dark sesame oil
½ cup minced scallions (pale green parts
   only)

In a large bowl, mix the flours and salt together. Add 1 tablespoon of canola oil and water, stirring to form a rough dough. The dough should be moist and springy but not sticky. If the dough seems too wet, knead in a little more flour. Turn the dough onto a lightly floured surface and knead about 5 minutes, until smooth. Cover and set aside for 30 minutes.

Turn the dough out onto a lightly floured surface and roll into a long snake about 1 inch in diameter. Cut the snake into 12 pieces. Roll out each piece into a circle about 5 inches in diameter. Brush the tops with sesame oil and sprinkle with scallions.

Roll up each circle into a snake, then coil it into a snail shape, making sure the seam is on the inside of the coil to help it stay closed. Secure the ends by pinching the dough together. Cover the pancakes and set aside for 30 minutes.

Finally, use a rolling pin to flatten each coil into a 4-inch circle.

Heat a large, deep skillet over high heat and add the ¾ cup canola oil. Heat the oven to 200 degrees and place an ovenproof dish inside to heat. When the oil is hot, add about 4 pancakes (you're cooking in batches to avoid crowding the pan), lower the heat to medium-high, and fry the pancakes until golden brown and crisp on both sides, about 2 minutes per side. Drain, sprinkle with salt, and transfer to the oven. The pancakes can be kept warm for up to 1 hour, but the sooner you serve them, the better they taste.

ORANGE *MU SHU* DUCK WITH CRANBERRY WILD RICE AND BRANDIED HOISIN SAUCE

MAKES
6 SERVINGS

I love to combine recipes from all over the world into one dish, making connections that weave all the flavors together. This irresistible dish is one I'm particularly proud of: a savory, aromatic combination of French duck à l'orange, the Chinese technique of using tangerine peel to perfume red meat, and distinctly American ingredients like wild rice and cranberries that are traditional with game. For the mu shu *I lightened the shreds of spiced duck with a toss of crunchy julienned vegetables. A side dish of juicy cranberries and nutty wild rice and a smoky hoisin sauce round out the flavor palette. I've provided a recipe for crêpes to wrap the* mu shu *in, but it is quite delicious without them as well.*

This duck dish is easy to make and has an extraordinary deep flavor. It really takes on the spice and citrus of the seasonings. But you can skip it altogether and use plain roast duck meat or even roast chicken in the recipe. In fact, leftover roast lamb and beef are good, too!

FOR THE DUCK:
6 whole duck legs
¼ cup Szechuan pepper salt (page 13)
¼ cup five-spice powder (page 4)
Freshly grated zest of 1 orange
2 cloves garlic, smashed
1 dried Thai bird chile (page 2) or fresh jalapeño chile
1 small bunch thyme sprigs
About 3 cups duck fat or canola oil

FOR THE SAUCE:
1 teaspoon canola oil
1 clove garlic, finely chopped
½ cup brandy
1 cup hoisin sauce (page 4)

TO FINISH THE DISH:
1 tablespoon canola oil
1 large onion, diced
1½ cups *each* julienned carrots, celery, red bell pepper, and sugar snap or snow peas
Freshly grated zest of 1 orange
Cranberry Wild Rice (recipe follows)
Crêpes (recipe follows; optional)
Cilantro sprigs and finely shredded scallions, for garnish

Prepare the duck: Generously season the legs with the pepper salt and five-spice powder. Rub in the orange zest, wrap or cover the legs, and refrigerate overnight. Rinse off the spices and pat dry. Heat the oven to 275 degrees. Place the legs in a roasting pan just big enough to hold them in a single layer. Add the garlic, chile, and thyme sprigs, strewing the thyme over the legs. Pour the fat over the legs until just covered. Cover tightly with aluminum foil and bake for 4 hours. Let cool in the pan. *(The duck can be prepared in advance and kept refrigerated up to 1 month.)*

Make the sauce: Heat the oil in a skillet over medium-high heat. Add the garlic and cook, stirring constantly, just until golden and fragrant. Turn off the heat and add the brandy, then whisk in the hoisin. Return the heat to medium and simmer until thick and saucy, 3 to 5 minutes. *(The sauce can be made in advance and kept refrigerated up to 1 week.)*

Prepare the *mu shu*: Heat the oven to 250 degrees. Lift the duck legs out of the pan, arrange in a roasting pan, and bake about 30 minutes, until the fat has rendered. When cool enough to handle, remove the duck meat from the bones and shred it coarsely. Heat the oil in a heavy skillet over medium-high heat. Add the onion and cook, stirring often, until the onion is softened and well browned, about 15 minutes. Add the vegetables and cook until hot but still crisp, about 3 minutes. Stir in the orange zest and duck meat.

Serve on cranberry wild rice and drizzle with brandied hoisin sauce. (Or, if using crêpes, roll the *mu shu* up in the crêpes and rest on the cranberry wild rice. Serve the sauce on the side for dipping.) Garnish with cilantro sprigs and shreds of scallion.

CRANBERRY WILD RICE

The tart, sweet cranberries here really tame the earthiness of the wild rice; green, anise-y tarragon lends a breath of freshness. This is excellent with any game dish or roast bird.

1 ½ cups wild rice
¾ cup dried cranberries
1 ½ cups ruby port
Kosher salt and freshly ground black
    pepper

4 teaspoons finely chopped tarragon or
    parsley

Bring a pot of salted water to a boil and cook the wild rice until very tender, about 40 minutes. Drain and place in a serving bowl.

Meanwhile, combine the cranberries and port in a saucepan and simmer until almost all the liquid has been absorbed. Pour over the wild rice and mix well. Season to taste with salt and pepper. Just before serving, reheat the rice, taste for salt and pepper, and mix in the tarragon.

CRÊPES

This is a basic Italian recipe for thin, tender crêpes, or crespelle. I have grown to pre-fer them to the floury Chinese pancakes used for mu shu.

1 cup milk
¾ cup all-purpose flour, sifted
2 eggs

⅛ teaspoon kosher salt
2 tablespoons unsalted butter

Whisk the milk and flour together until smooth. Whisk in the eggs, then the salt.

Melt a teaspoon of butter in an 8-inch nonstick skillet over medium heat. Stir the batter and pour 2 tablespoons of it into the pan. Swirl the pan so that the bat-ter evenly coats the bottom. Let cook until the bottom is dry and lightly browned, then flip with a spatula and cook on the other side. Remove to a plate. Repeat with the remaining butter and batter, stirring it each time before pouring it into the pan. Stack the crêpes as they are done and set aside at room temperature until ready to serve.

CRISPY DUCK SCHNITZEL WITH HAZELNUT BROWN BUTTER AND BEET, ORANGE, AND ARUGULA SALAD

MAKES
4 SERVINGS

Crisp-fried cutlets—tonkatsu—are one of the most popular street foods in Japan. Japanese cooks have raised deep-frying to a high art with panko, the lightest bread crumbs, which have recently become available in this country. I've always liked tonkatsu (and its near cousins Wiener schnitzel and fried chicken) for its crunchy outside and tender meat, and as soon I applied the panko crust to a flavorful duck breast, I knew I was on to something big. As it turns out, the dish is one of the most popular entrées at Restaurant AZ. The nutty browned butter sauce, freshened with orange, really sets off the "schnitzel." And the cool, tangy salad completes the plate and keeps the rest of the dish from feeling too rich.

4 duck breast halves, skinned and
   excess fat trimmed off
Kosher salt and freshly ground black
   pepper
2 eggs
½ cup freshly grated Parmesan cheese
½ cup mixed chopped herbs, such as
   parsley, mint, cilantro, and thyme
2 cups bread crumbs, preferably *panko*
   (see above; available at Asian markets)

About 8 tablespoons (1 stick) butter
¼ cup chopped toasted hazelnuts
   (page 11)
Grated zest and juice of 2 oranges
Snipped chives, for garnish
Beet, Orange, and Arugula Salad
   (recipe follows)

Butterfly the duck breasts: Place a breast on a work surface and place your hand on top of it. Using a sharp knife, horizontally (with the knife parallel to the work surface) cut the breast almost in half, leaving the 2 halves attached along 1 edge. Open up the butterflied breast and place it between 2 sheets of plastic wrap. Using a mallet or a heavy skillet, pound gently, starting at the thick center and working your way out to the edge, until the breast is about ¼ inch thick or less all over. Season with salt and pepper. Repeat with the remaining breasts, stacking the pounded breasts between sheets of waxed paper until ready to cook. *(The recipe can be made in advance up to this point and kept refrigerated up to 1 day.)*

Whisk the eggs, cheese, and herbs together. Spread the bread crumbs on a large plate. Heat the oven to 200 degrees and place an ovenproof platter inside to warm.

Heat a large skillet over high heat (work in batches or use 2 skillets if necessary to avoid crowding). Dip 1 breast in the egg mixture, then dredge on both sides in bread crumbs. Add 2 tablespoons of butter to the skillet and add the breast. Cook until golden brown and crisp, about 4 to 5 minutes (do not let the butter or the coating burn and blacken). Turn and cook briefly on the other side

just until browned, adding more butter if needed. Remove the cooked breasts from the pan and keep warm in the oven.

To make the sauce, add 2 tablespoons of butter to the hot skillet you cooked the duck in and melt over high heat. Watch carefully to let the butter solids toast slightly, just until they turn light brown and the mixture smells nutty. Add the hazelnuts and orange zest, and cook, stirring, for 1 minute. Remove the pan from the heat and add the orange juice. Return the pan to the heat and let boil until reduced to a sauce. Season with salt and pepper.

To serve, place a duck breast on a serving plate and top with the sauce. Sprinkle with chives. Serve immediately with beet, orange, and arugula salad.

BEET, ORANGE, AND ARUGULA SALAD

MAKES
4 SERVINGS

Red and yellow beets tossed with green arugula make for a spectacularly colorful plate. The salad is quite peppery and piquant with vinegar, and freshened with orange juice and chives—a perfect contrast to fried food or any rich dish. If you want to make it truly luxurious, drizzle on a little truffle oil. Beets and truffles are a lovely combination.

3 large red beets (do not peel)
3 large yellow beets (do not peel)
1 shallot, minced
2 tablespoons chopped chives
3 cups arugula

¼ cup orange juice
1 ½ teaspoons sherry vinegar
Kosher salt and freshly ground black
   pepper

Roast the beets: Heat the oven to 350 degrees. In separate roasting pans or wrapped separately in aluminum foil (to prevent the colors from bleeding onto each other), roast the beets until tender when pierced with a knife, about 30 minutes, depending on the size of the beets. When cool enough to handle, peel and dice into bite-size cubes. *(The recipe can be made in advance up to this point and kept refrigerated up to 1 day.)* Bring to room temperature before serving.

Just before serving, toss the diced beets with the shallot, chives, arugula, orange juice, and vinegar. Season to taste with salt and pepper.

CRISPED DUCK BREAST WITH LEMONGRASS GLAZE AND SWEET POTATO-COCONUT PUREE

In New York, caramel is very popular on dessert menus—but I think mine is the only restaurant that uses it in entrées, too. Simmering food in caramel, a molten hot blend of sugar and water, is a traditional cooking method that I learned in Southeast Asia. The addition of salty fish sauce and bracing lemongrass gives the caramel depth of flavor and keeps it from being just sweet.

In this recipe, the caramel (sparked with my additions of ginger, shallots, and chile heat) acts as a flavor-packed marinade for meaty duck breasts. It also helps the duck skin to become incredibly crisp. A smooth, luxurious puree is the perfect side dish.

FOR THE GLAZE:

1 stalk lemongrass, tough ends trimmed off and discarded
2 cloves garlic, peeled
2 slices fresh ginger (do not peel)
1 shallot, roughly chopped
1 jalapeño chile, roughly chopped
½ cup sugar
¼ cup fish sauce (page 3)

TO FINISH THE DISH:

4 duck breast halves, with the skin on
2 tablespoons canola oil
½ cup red wine
Sweet Potato–Coconut Puree (recipe follows)
Dried Cranberry and Kumquat Chutney (page 28) *or* Simple Herb Salad (page 58)
Cilantro sprigs and finely shredded scallions, for garnish

Make the glaze: Thinly slice the lemongrass and place in a food processor. Add the garlic and ginger, and pulse just until coarsely ground. Add the shallot and jalapeño, and process until finely ground.

Pour the sugar into a medium-size heavy saucepan and turn the heat to medium-high. Cook, breaking up any lumps with a wooden spoon, until the sugar melts and turns amber, about 5 minutes. Add the lemongrass mixture and cook, stirring constantly, for 1 minute (the mixture will seize up at first and then smooth out). Carefully pour in the fish sauce and simmer to blend, about 30 seconds. Remove

from the heat and let cool to room temperature. *(The glaze can be made in advance and kept refrigerated indefinitely.)*

Score the fatty skin of the duck breasts with a sharp knife, cutting a crosshatch pattern all over the skin (this will help release the fat under the skin as the breasts cook). Place in a shallow dish, pour in the glaze, and set aside to marinate at least 15 minutes or, refrigerated, up to 12 hours.

Heat the oil in a large, heavy skillet over high heat. Add the duck breasts to the pan, skin side down, then lower the heat to very low (this will slowly render the fat and prevent the caramel from burning). Cook about 10 to 15 minutes, checking often after the first 5 minutes.

Meanwhile, heat the oven to 350 degrees. When the fat has rendered and the skin is golden brown, crisp, and thin, pour off all the fat. Add the red wine to the hot pan, turn the breasts over, and bake for 5 to 10 minutes, or until the red wine is a thick glaze. Let rest for 5 minutes, then slice against the grain and serve with sweet potato–coconut puree and dried cranberry and kumquat chutney. Garnish with cilantro sprigs and shreds of scallion.

SWEET POTATO-COCONUT PUREE

MAKES 4 TO 6 SERVINGS

Simple, yes, but so good. Nutmeg adds a subtle but very welcome spicy edge to this sweet, smooth puree. Sweet potatoes and coconut milk make a traditional soup in Laos, but this also has a very American, Thanksgiving-y flavor and feel.

1 (14-ounce) can coconut milk
6 large sweet potatoes, peeled and cut
   into large chunks

Freshly grated nutmeg
Kosher salt and freshly ground black
   pepper

Pour the coconut milk into a saucepan and simmer until reduced by one-fourth.

Meanwhile, boil the sweet potatoes in a large pot of boiling salted water until very tender. Drain very well and transfer to a food processor or mixer. Add the coconut milk and a few gratings of nutmeg, and pulse together just until smooth. Season to taste with nutmeg, salt, and pepper, and serve hot.

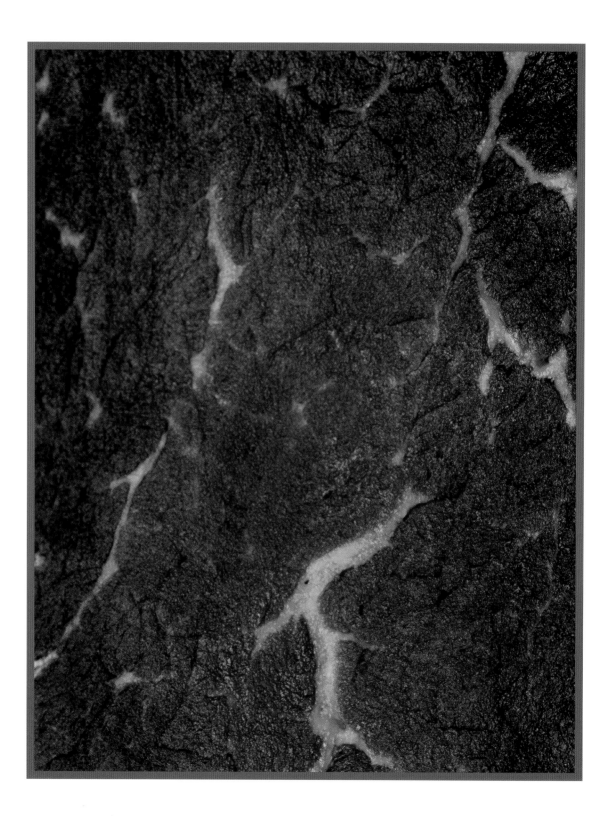

Meat Main Courses

PORK WITH FORTY CLOVES OF GARLIC

CHINESE FIVE-SPICED SPARERIBS

LONG-ROASTED HONEY-GLAZED PORK WITH
ONION MARMALADE

APPLE-BRINED PORK CHOPS WITH TEA-
ARMAGNAC PRUNES AND SAUTÉED NAPA
CABBAGE

VIETNAMESE BARBECUED BEEF AND FRESH
MINT WRAPPED IN RICE PAPER

GRILLED BEEF WRAPS AND CHINESE LONG
BEANS WITH GARLIC OIL AND SESAME SALT

MALAYSIAN BEEF *RENDANG* WITH DRY
COCONUT, SHALLOTS, AND COCONUT RICE

THAI BEEF STEW WITH RED CURRY

MISO-BRAISED SHORT RIBS WITH SHERRY-
CARAMEL–GLAZED ONIONS AND BRAISED
BROCCOLI RABE

LAMB SMOTHERED IN CARAMELIZED ONIONS
AND SPICES WITH PARSLEY AND SWEET
ONION SALAD

ROAST BONELESS LEG OF LAMB WITH SPICY
CUMIN CRUST

LAMB WITH SPICED *KORMA* SAUCE AND
CHAPPATIS

MALAYSIAN *SATAY* PARTY WITH SESAME-
CUCUMBER SALAD

PORK WITH FORTY CLOVES OF GARLIC

Chicken with forty cloves of garlic is one of the towering classics of the French kitchen. But having grown up in a Chinese household, when I think of that much garlic, I think of pork. Pork and garlic, like fish and ginger, are one of the key flavor pairs in Chinese cooking—though 40 cloves is an unprecedented amount! I use 20 cloves to simmer the pork, then I roast the other 20 until sweet and aromatic, and toss them with the rustic bean and vegetable ragout I like to serve alongside.

It is best to use a fatty cut of pork like the shoulder or belly for this recipe, because it cooks for about 3 hours. The fat and cartilage melt slowly away, leaving tender, juicy meat behind.

FOR THE PORK:

3½ to 4 pounds boneless pork belly or pork shoulder (see the note on page 178; do not trim off exterior fat)
½ cup five-spice powder (page 4)
Kosher salt and freshly ground black pepper
1 onion, peeled
1 carrot, peeled
2 stalks celery
4 bay leaves
1 large sprig fresh thyme
About 3 quarts lightly salted Chicken Stock (page 13) or canned broth
20 cloves garlic, peeled

TO FINISH THE DISH:

20 cloves garlic, peeled
3 tablespoons canola oil
Kosher salt and freshly ground black pepper
1 cup *each* diced carrots, celery, leeks, and onions
1 cup cooking liquid from the pork
2½ cups cooked white beans
½ cup finely chopped parsley
¼ cup *each* finely chopped fresh sage and fresh thyme

At least 2 days before serving, begin the pork: Using the tip of a sharp knife, cut a pattern of crosshatches about ⅛ inch deep all over the outside of the pork. Rub the pork all over with five-spice powder, place it in a glass or ceramic dish, cover, and refrigerate overnight.

The next day, bring the pork to room temperature. Season it all over with salt and pepper and transfer to a deep pot. Add the onion, carrot, celery, bay leaves, and thyme. Pour in enough chicken stock to cover by about 4 inches, adding water if needed. Bring to a boil, lower the heat, and simmer gently for 3 hours, adding the garlic for the last 30 minutes of cooking time. The fat should be skimmed off the top every 15 minutes or so, using a ladle. Let cool and refrigerate overnight. (*The recipe can be made in advance up to this point and kept refrigerated up to 3 days.*)

When ready to serve, lift off and discard the fat on top of the liquid. Rewarm the meat in the liquid.

Make the vegetables: Preheat the oven (or a toaster oven) to 400 degrees. Rub the garlic cloves with 1 tablespoon of the oil on a large square of aluminum foil. Sprinkle with salt and pepper, wrap tightly, and bake until very soft and sweet, about 40 minutes. Heat the remaining 2 tablespoons oil in a skillet over high heat. Add the carrots, celery, leeks, and onions, and cook, stirring, until the onions are softened and translucent, about 5 minutes. Add the cooking liquid and cook until the vegetables are tender, about 10 minutes. Add the beans, lower the heat, and simmer until only a little bit of liquid remains in the pot. Fold in the roasted garlic and chopped herbs and season to taste with salt and pepper.

When ready to serve, drain the pork and discard all the liquid and vegetables in the pot. Slice the pork and serve with the bean-vegetable mixture.

CHINESE FIVE-SPICED SPARERIBS

I love real barbecued ribs, but making them in a New York City kitchen (even a state-of-the-art restaurant one) is virtually impossible. So I devised this alternate method for cooking ribs that are rich, spicy, and so tender they fall off the bone. The flavors of five-spice powder, hoisin sauce, ginger, and soy permeate the ribs as they simmer. They can be prepared days beforehand even up until the final broiling to heat them through and crisp the skin.

I know it seems odd to fry the ribs before simmering them, but the crust that forms really helps to seal in the juices. Serve the ribs as a snack or as an entrée with Cold Spicy Sesame Noodles (page 42) and a salad of watercress, red onion, and Napa cabbage tossed with Soy-Lime Vinaigrette (page 59).

Canola oil for frying
8 to 10 meaty pork spareribs, cut into approximately 3-inch lengths (your butcher can do this for you)
2½ cups lightly salted Chicken Stock (page 13) or canned broth
1½ teaspoons five-spice powder (page 4)

½ teaspoon sugar
½ cup hoisin sauce (page 4)
2 teaspoons miso (page 6), any kind
¼ cup rice wine (page 7)
3 cloves garlic, chopped
¼ cup chopped fresh ginger (no need to peel it)
2 tablespoons soy sauce

Heat 3 to 4 inches of oil in a deep, heavy pot over high heat until it ripples. Working in batches to avoid crowding the pan, fry the ribs on both sides until golden brown and crisp. Drain on paper towels or brown paper bags.

In a large pot, combine all the remaining ingredients. Add the ribs, then add water to the pot until the ribs are just covered. Bring to a boil, lower the heat, and simmer, uncovered, for 45 minutes, or until tender. *(The recipe can be cooled to room temperature and then kept refrigerated in the cooking liquid up to 3 days.)*

Just before serving, heat a broiler to high. Lift the ribs out of the liquid and broil just until browned, crisp, and heated through. Serve immediately.

LONG-ROASTED HONEY-GLAZED PORK WITH ONION MARMALADE

MAKES
4 TO 6
SERVINGS

Everyone loves Chinese roast pork, and one of my first missions as a chef was to re-create that glorious combination of savory, tender meat and crisp, salty-sweet skin. Roasting a pork belly may seem odd at first, but you'll see that the slow cooking melts all the excess fat out of the meat and creates the perfect glaze on the outside. Pork is bred to be so lean now that I actually prefer to cook with the fattier cuts; other cuts dry out almost immediately. You can order the pork belly from your butcher.

The onion marmalade that cooks along with the pork is so soft and sweet that it qualifies as a fragrant sauce. I like to wrap them together in Scallion Pancakes (page 159).

1 (3- to 4-pound) pork belly
  (see note above)
3 cups honey
1 cup soy sauce
½ cup ancho chile powder
½ cup five-spice powder (page 4)
15 onions, thinly sliced

4 fresh or dried bay leaves
2 cups white wine, lightly salted Chicken
  Stock (page 13), or water
Finely shredded scallions, for garnish
Basic Rice (page 10) or Scallion Pancakes
  (page 159)
Brandied Hoisin Sauce (page 161)

Bring a large pot of water to a boil. Rinse the pork belly and pat dry. Using a very strong, sharp knife (I use a box cutter), score the skin with a crosshatch pattern into 1-inch squares. Put the belly in a colander, skin side up. Slowly pour the boiling water over the belly to melt off some of the fat (this will help the skin crisp up).

Heat the honey in a saucepan. Stir in the soy sauce, ancho powder, and five-spice powder. Heat the mixture through and then remove from the heat.

Heat the oven to 250 degrees. Combine the onions and bay leaves in a large roasting pan. Brush the pork with the warm honey mixture, then place in the roasting pan on top of the onions. Pour the wine into the pan.

Roast the pork for 4 1/2 hours, brushing with honey glaze and stirring the onions every 30 minutes. Raise the heat to 400 degrees and roast without basting for another 30 minutes. Set the pork aside to rest and pour off any liquid from the onion mixture in the roasting pan. Remove any scorched bits of onion and discard.

Slice the pork 1/2 inch thick for serving and sprinkle with scallions. The pork and onion marmalade can be served over rice, drizzled with hoisin sauce, or wrapped together in scallion pancakes dabbed with hoisin sauce.

APPLE-BRINED PORK CHOPS WITH TEA-ARMAGNAC PRUNES AND SAUTÉED NAPA CABBAGE

MAKES
4 SERVINGS

FALL / WINTER

Roast pork with fruit is just one of those perfect combinations, a gift from the flavor gods. Dried fruit has an intensity and a tartness that I love (the flavor is totally different from and much more complex than fresh fruit), and I use it often in savory dishes. You'll need to prepare the prunes at least a week ahead. The overnight brining makes pork juicy and flavorful.

Prunes with Armagnac is a classic combination from southwest France, emphasizing both the rich, raisiny sweetness of the wine and the deep, aged flavor of the fruit. The longer you keep the prunes, the better they will taste. Serve this dish with mashed potatoes and Sautéed Napa Cabbage.

FOR THE PRUNES:
1 cup Armagnac, cognac, or another brandy
1 cup strong brewed tea
½ cup sugar
1 (3-inch) cinnamon stick
1 strip orange zest
12 pitted prunes

FOR THE PORK CHOPS:
1 apple, not too tart, peeled and coarsely chopped
1 small onion, coarsely chopped
3 cups apple juice
Kosher salt
5 black peppercorns
1 (3-inch) cinnamon stick
1 star anise pod
1 bay leaf
4 large center-cut loin pork chops, about 2 inches thick
1 tablespoon canola oil
Kosher salt and freshly ground black pepper
Cilantro sprigs, for garnish
Sautéed Napa Cabbage (recipe follows)

At least a week before serving, make the prunes: Combine the Armagnac, tea, sugar, cinnamon stick, and orange zest in a small pot and bring to a simmer, stirring often to dissolve the sugar. Meanwhile, put the prunes in a heatproof container or bowl, small enough that the prunes will be completely covered by the liquid. Pour the hot liquid over the prunes, let cool to room temperature, cover, and refrigerate for at least a week.

The day before serving, begin the pork chops: Combine the apple, onion, apple

juice, 2 tablespoons salt, peppercorns, cinnamon, star anise, and bay leaf in a medium pot and bring to a boil. Remove from the heat and let the brine mixture cool to room temperature. Arrange the pork chops in a deep baking dish (not aluminum) just large enough to hold the chops in 1 layer. Pour the brine mixture over the meat and cover tightly with plastic wrap. Refrigerate overnight, up to 24 hours, turning once.

When ready to serve, heat the oven to 450 degrees and remove the prunes from the refrigerator. Remove the chops from the brine mixture and pat dry. Season generously with pepper and lightly with salt.

Heat a heavy ovenproof skillet (preferably cast iron) over high heat. Add the oil and swirl to coat. When the oil is almost smoking, add the chops and lower the heat to medium-high. Sear until golden brown, 2 to 3 minutes per side. Transfer the pan to the hot oven and roast another 7 minutes, until the meat feels firm but springy when you press it and the meat near the bone is still barely pink. Remove from the oven and let rest in the hot pan for 5 minutes. Serve immediately, using a slotted spoon to place a couple of prunes alongside each chop. Garnish with cilantro sprigs and serve with sautéed Napa cabbage.

Sautéed Napa Cabbage

MAKES
4 SERVINGS

¼ cup diced bacon
2 cloves garlic, minced
4 cups shredded Napa or savoy
   cabbage

¼ cup lightly salted Chicken Stock
   (page 13) or canned broth
Kosher salt and freshly ground black
   pepper

In a skillet, heat the bacon over high heat. When the white fat turns to liquid and the bacon pieces are golden, add the garlic and cook, stirring, until golden. Stir in the cabbage and the stock. Bring to a simmer, cover, and simmer until very tender, about 20 minutes. For the last minute of cooking, uncover and raise the heat to high to evaporate the cooking liquid. Season to taste with salt and pepper and serve hot.

Vietnamese Barbecued Beef and Fresh Mint Wrapped in Rice Paper

MAKES
4 TO 6
SERVINGS

My favorite thing about Vietnamese cooking is its bold use of fresh herbs such as mint, basil, and cilantro. Instead of a timid sprinkling of minced leaves, Vietnamese cooks present platters of whole sprigs, to be stirred into soups, tossed into salads, and wrapped around hot spring rolls or grilled meat for maximum contrast. This dish is a fairly traditional dinner, simple, tasty, and fun to eat. The meat is deliciously seasoned with a lively combination of lemongrass and garlic. (Leaving out the meat makes for a delicious vegetarian version, as pictured.)

Once you've purchased the rice papers (they're available at Asian grocers), working with them is very easy; they are not as fragile as they look.

FOR THE MEAT:
1 ½ to 2 pounds beefsteak, such as strip, shell, skirt, hanger, flank, or sirloin
1 stalk lemongrass, tough ends trimmed off and remainder finely chopped
1 clove garlic, minced
1 teaspoon fish sauce (page 3)

FOR THE SAUCE:
6 tablespoons fish sauce (page 3)
2 teaspoons sugar
Freshly grated zest and freshly squeezed juice of 1 lime
1 or 2 jalapeño chiles, seeded and finely chopped
1 carrot, grated

FOR SERVING:
1 cup mint sprigs
1 cup cilantro sprigs
½ cup basil sprigs (preferably Thai basil)
1 head Boston, butter, or Bibb lettuce, leaves separated and left whole
1 red bell pepper, cut into thin strips
32 pieces rice paper (see note above)
Kosher salt
Splash of rice vinegar
2 teaspoons sesame seeds, toasted (page 12)

Prepare the meat: Wrap the whole steak in plastic wrap and put it in the freezer for 45 minutes to firm up. Slice the meat very thin across the grain. Lay the slices in

overlapping rows on a large platter. Sprinkle the slices with lemongrass, garlic, and fish sauce. Let marinate for 30 minutes before cooking.

Make the sauce: Combine all the ingredients in a bowl. Before serving, divide into individual bowls for dipping.

Arrange the herbs and vegetables on a platter and refrigerate until ready to serve.

Shortly before serving, prepare the rice paper: Pour 2 inches of hot water into a shallow bowl. Season with salt and a splash of rice vinegar. Dip each piece of rice paper in the water for about 45 seconds to soften, then lift out, shake off excess water, fold the paper into quarters, and place on a serving platter lined with a clean kitchen towel. Cover with a clean damp towel until ready to serve.

Heat a grill to its hottest point. Grill the beef slices very briefly, just until well browned on both sides (depending on how thin your slices are, the meat will be cooked through after 30 seconds to 2 minutes per side).

To serve, each person makes his or her own rolls of beef, herbs, and vegetables, sprinkled with sesame seeds and wrapped in rice paper. Dip into sauce.

GRILLED BEEF WRAPS AND CHINESE LONG BEANS WITH GARLIC OIL AND SESAME SALT

If you love to grill, this method is fabulously easy and really fun for a party. People love to make their own wraps, choosing just the perfect combination of smoky grilled beef, fragrant steamed rice, and spicy sauce to roll in a crisp green lettuce leaf. To slice the beef very thin (as though for cheese steaks), I freeze the meat to firm it up. Then I lay the slices out on sheets of paper and brush them with marinade so they're completely ready to go. When it's time to cook, you simply lay the meat on the grill, peel off the paper, and it's cooked!

This simple dipping sauce is used constantly in Thailand and Vietnam, where each person at the table mixes his or her own private blend of pungent fish sauce, tangy lime juice, hot chile, and sugar. You can serve the other suggested sauces in addition (or instead) and any little salads or cooked vegetables that you prefer.

FOR THE MEAT:
2 pounds boneless ribeye, skirt, strip, or
   hanger steak
½ cup *shiro* miso (page 6)
½ cup mirin (page 5)
¼ cup canola oil
2 tablespoons sugar

FOR THE SAUCE:
1 clove garlic, minced
¼ cup fish sauce (page 3)
¼ cup lime juice
¼ cup water
¼ cup grated carrot
1 small jalapeño chile, seeded and minced
Sugar

TO FINISH THE DISH:
About 24 large leaves of Boston or
   iceberg lettuce
About 3 cups cooked white rice
1 cup Brandied Hoisin Sauce (page 161;
   optional)
1 cup Aromatic Tomato–Black Bean Sauce
   (page 115; optional)
Chinese Long Beans with Garlic Oil and
   Sesame Salt (recipe follows)
Cucumber, Red Pepper, and Peanut Salad
   (page 60; optional)
Crunchy Bean Sprout Salad with Sesame
   and *Sambal* (page 61; optional)

Prepare the meat: Wrap the whole steak in plastic wrap and put it in the freezer for 1 hour. (This will make it firm and easy to slice.) Meanwhile, mix the miso, mirin, oil, and sugar together in a bowl.

Make the sauce: Stir all the ingredients together and add sugar to taste. Divide in individual dipping bowls for serving.

Lay out a piece of parchment paper next to a work surface. Place the cold steak on the surface and slice it very thin, about 1/8 inch thick. Arrange the slices in a single layer on the paper. If necessary, cover the first layer of meat with another piece of paper and continue until all the meat is sliced. Refrigerate until ready to cook.

When ready to cook, heat a grill to very hot. Thickly brush the top layer of meat with the miso mixture, leaving the meat on the paper. Lift up the paper with the meat attached and quickly place it, meat side down, on the hot grill. Peel off the paper, leaving the meat on the grill. By the time you have peeled off the paper, the meat will be almost cooked; it should take 30 seconds to 1 minute for rare meat. Without turning the slices over, remove the cooked steak to a platter. Repeat with the remaining meat. Do not overcook the meat, or it will toughen.

To serve, wrap the steak and rice together in a lettuce leaf and dip it in the sauce (or sauces). Pass the salads and vegetables separately.

Chinese Long Beans with Garlic Oil and Sesame Salt

MAKES
4 TO 6
SERVINGS

Chinese long beans really are long—they can grow up to 3 feet and are sold in Asian greengrocers tied in knots or coiled up in loops. They're actually the pods of black-eyed peas. Long beans are firmer and thicker than our green beans and have a wilder flavor, but you can certainly use green beans here. Try to find rather mature ones so that the dish isn't too sweet. Broccoli rabe would also be a good substitute.

1 tablespoon sesame seeds, toasted
  (page 12)
2 teaspoons kosher salt
¼ cup canola oil

4 cloves garlic, minced
1 Thai bird chile, crushed (page 2)
1½ pounds Chinese long beans or string
  beans, cut into 1-inch lengths

In a blender or spice grinder, grind the sesame seeds and salt together until fine. Set aside.

Heat a heavy skillet (with a lid) over high heat. Add the oil and heat. Stir in the garlic and chile, and cook, stirring, just until golden and fragrant. Stir in the beans, lower the heat to medium-low, cover, and cook just until tender, about 5 minutes. The beans will steam in their own liquid, but if you are afraid they may burn, add a tablespoon of water to the pan. Serve hot or at room temperature, sprinkled with the sesame salt.

MALAYSIAN BEEF *RENDANG* WITH DRY COCONUT, SHALLOTS, AND COCONUT RICE

The cooking of Malaysia, where I lived as a child, is a delicious brew of Southeast Asia, India, and China—with some distinctively Malaysian ingredients and dishes. Rendang is one of those, and it's the kind of dish that stays with you for the rest of your life, wherever you go and whatever you cook! I've never encountered this method of cooking anywhere else. The meat is simmered in coconut milk, dry coconut, chiles, and shallots until all the liquid disappears and the meat is infused with its flavors. Then it is stir-fried in the coconut oil that remains. The finished dish is rich and spicy. When I was little, we used to have it as a special treat, served on plates of banana leaves, with crisp cucumber slices for contrast.

1 pound unsweetened dry coconut

10 mixed dried chiles, such as Thai bird (page 2), guajillo, and ancho, soaked at least 2 hours or overnight, drained, seeded, and stemmed

4 cups coarsely chopped shallots

2½ pounds beef stew meat, cut into 1-inch pieces

2 kaffir lime leaves (page 4)

2 stalks lemongrass, tough ends trimmed off and tender stalks cut into 3-inch lengths and smashed

2 (2-inch) pieces galangal (page 4) or fresh ginger

5 cups coconut milk

Kosher salt and freshly ground black pepper

Coconut Rice (recipe follows) or Basic Rice (page 10) for serving

Heat the oven to 325 degrees. Spread the coconut out on a large sheet pan and toast, stirring every 8 to 10 minutes, until golden and fragrant, about 25 minutes.

In a food processor, combine 2 tablespoons of toasted coconut with the soaked chiles and the shallots. Puree to a paste and transfer to a large, heavy pot. Add the beef and toss to coat well. Place the pot over medium-high heat and add the lime leaves, lemongrass, galangal, coconut milk, salt, and pepper. When the mixture comes to a boil, lower the heat and simmer about 30 minutes, or until the meat is tender. Stir occasionally.

Once the meat is tender, raise the heat to medium-high. Reduce the *rendang*: Stir constantly until the coconut oil starts to separate from the sauce and the sauce is thick and fairly dry (this may take up to 30 minutes). The coconut will be browned and toasty, and the dish will be dry, not too saucy. Taste for salt and pepper, and serve with rice.

Coconut Rice

This recipe may look as though it's for a dessert, but it actually has only a hint of sweetness. The vanilla brings out the creamy coconut flavor, making the rice a perfect foil for spicy curries.

2½ cups basmati rice
2 cups coconut milk
1 vanilla bean, split lengthwise

Pinch of kosher salt
Pinch of sugar

Combine all the ingredients in a heavy saucepan with a tight-fitting lid. Pour in water until the liquid is about ¾ inch above the rice. (You can test it by waiting for the rice to settle, then placing your fingertip on the top of the rice. The liquid should come to the first joint of your finger.) Bring to a boil over high heat, then cover, lower the heat, and simmer undisturbed for 20 minutes. Turn off the heat and let sit undisturbed for 10 minutes. Use chopsticks or a large fork to fluff the rice. Keep covered until ready to serve; the rice is good hot or at room temperature.

Thai Beef Stew with Red Curry

When it comes to cooking at home, I'm something of a meat-and-potatoes person. I love to fill my house with the rich perfumes of stews and curries. This irresistible dish is my combination of a classic winy French beef stew and a beef curry napped with a sauce of spices and aromatics. Red curry paste is a key ingredient in Thai kitchens. It's a homemade or store-bought mixture of cilantro roots and seeds, garlic, shallots, lime leaves, and plenty of the dried chiles that make the paste glow red. I find it bracing and aromatic but not too fiery.

Like all stews, this one is best if you cook it a day ahead and refrigerate it overnight before serving. I use top round of beef because the slow cooking breaks down the meat into tender, flavorful chunks. The banana gives the sauce body and sweetness, but if it seems too odd, you can leave it out.

2 tablespoons canola oil
5 large onions, chopped
2 stalks celery, chopped
1 yellow plantain, peeled with a sharp
   knife and cut into 1-inch chunks, *or*
   1 peeled banana
2 medium-size russet (baking) potatoes,
   peeled and cut into 1/2-inch pieces
2 tablespoons red curry paste
   (page 3)

2 cups red wine
2½ pounds top round of beef or flank,
   skirt, sirloin, or hanger steak, cut into
   1½-inch pieces
2 cups lightly salted Beef Stock
   (page 14), Chicken Stock (page 13),
   canned broth, or water
Fish sauce (page 3)
Basic Rice (page 10), preferably jasmine
Cilantro leaves, for garnish

Heat the oil in a large pot over high heat. Add the onions and celery. Cook over high heat, stirring, until the vegetables are softened and lightly browned, about 10 minutes. Add the plantain and potatoes, and mix well.

Add the curry paste to the pot and cook, stirring, for 5 minutes. Pour the wine into the pan and boil until the liquid is reduced by half. Add the meat and stock, bring to a boil, and lower the heat to a simmer. Cover and simmer for 30 minutes.

Add the potatoes and simmer 15 minutes more, or until the potatoes are tender. (If the stew seems soupy when you add the potatoes, uncover the pot for this part of the cooking; if not, keep it covered.)

The stew can be served immediately, but it tastes even better if you refrigerate it overnight, skim off the fat, and reheat before serving. Before serving, taste for saltiness. If the stew needs salt, season with fish sauce. Serve on a bed of rice, garnished with cilantro.

Miso-Braised Short Ribs with Sherry-Caramel-Glazed Onions and Braised Broccoli Rabe

FALL/WINTER

Slow-braised short ribs are the best kind of home cooking: easy, savory, inexpensive, and so aromatic that you build up an appetite over hours as the wonderful savory smells fill and warm your house. This is real rib-sticking, cold-weather cooking.

I often use miso in my stews to transform the sauce into a thick, velvety glaze. Miso is a puree of soybeans, salt, and grain, fermented to a rich, tangy flavor. Depending on the grain that is used, miso can be almost white to deep brown. For this recipe, golden shiro miso made with rice is my choice. Serve it on a bed of Taro Gnocchi, soft noodles, or mashed potatoes to soak up the unmissable sauce.

FOR THE RIBS:

6 pounds beef short ribs, cut into 2 × 6-inch pieces (your butcher can do this)
Kosher salt and freshly ground black pepper
1 tablespoon canola oil
1 onion, chopped
1 carrot, chopped
2 celery stalks, chopped
1 cup *each* red wine, rice wine (page 7), and plum wine (page 6), or use 3 cups red wine
½ cup *shiro* miso (page 6)
About 3 cups lightly salted Chicken Stock (page 13) or canned broth or water

FOR THE ONIONS:

1 tablespoon butter
30 pearl onions, peeled (frozen pearl onions are fine)
¼ cup sherry vinegar
2 tablespoons sugar

TO FINISH THE DISH:

Braised Broccoli Rabe (recipe follows)
Taro Gnocchi (recipe follows)
Cilantro sprigs, for garnish

Season the ribs all over with salt and pepper. Heat the oil in a large, heavy skillet over high heat until hot but not smoking. Working in batches if necessary to avoid crowding the pan, sear the ribs until well browned on both sides. Remove them from the skillet as they brown.

When all the ribs are browned and the pan is empty, drain off any excess fat in the pan and heat the oven to 300 degrees. Add the onion, carrot, and celery to the pan and cook, stirring, until softened and browned, about 10 minutes. Add the wines, bring to a boil, and boil for 5 minutes to evaporate the alcohol. Whisk in the miso. Return the ribs to the pan and pour in the stock until the ribs are just covered with liquid, adding water if needed. Bring to a boil, cover the pot tightly with a lid or aluminum foil, and bake at least 2 hours or more, until the meat is very tender.

Cook the onions: Melt the butter in a heavy skillet over high heat. When it foams, add the onions and cook, stirring, until softened and lightly browned, 5 to 10 minutes (frozen onions are precooked and will soften quickly). Add the vinegar and sugar, turn the heat to low, and cook until the onions are glazed and the syrup is caramelized. If the onions are not yet tender, add a bit of water and keep cooking until they are.

When the meat is tender, lift the ribs out of the liquid and set aside. Strain the liquid into a clean pot. Mash the vegetables until smooth with a potato masher or a ricer and stir back into the braising liquid. Simmer until reduced by half. Season to taste with salt and pepper.

When ready to serve, gently reheat the ribs in the reduced liquid. Garnish with cilantro and serve with the glazed onions, broccoli rabe, and taro *gnocchi*.

Braised Broccoli Rabe

MAKES
4 TO 6
SERVINGS

I don't know what I'd do without this simple dish of peppery broccoli rabe; it makes the perfect side for so many of my dishes. Try it with any roast or stew. It's very easy to make, and the flavors are always fresh and lively.

2 (1-pound) bunches broccoli rabe
2 tablespoons canola oil
2 cloves garlic, minced
1 Thai bird chile, crushed (page 2)

1 tablespoon fish sauce (page 3)
¼ cup lightly salted Chicken Stock
    (page 13), canned broth, or water

Remove the leaves and thick center stems from the broccoli rabe and discard. Cut the broccoli rabe into reasonably even florets.

In a heavy pot, heat the oil over high heat. Add the garlic and chile, and cook just until fragrant, stirring constantly to prevent the garlic from browning. Add the broccoli rabe, fish sauce, and stock. Bring to a simmer and cook, covered, for 5 to 8 minutes, until very tender. Serve hot.

Taro Gnocchi

Italian gnocchi, potato dumplings, make wonderfully absorbent little pillows for sauces. I set out to transform the recipe for AZ and found that a sprinkling of five-spice powder and the addition of taro, a starchy Asian root vegetable, gave my recipe just the right lightness. You can buy taros at Asian and Caribbean markets. I love these with stews, but you can also buy frozen or vacuum-packed gnocchi from Italy, available in many stores these days.

I pound taros, scrubbed
I pound baking potatoes, scrubbed
¼ teaspoon five-spice powder
   (page 4)
Freshly grated nutmeg

Kosher salt
3 egg yolks
About ½ cup all-purpose flour
6 tablespoons unsalted butter

Make the *gnocchi*: Heat the oven to 350 degrees. Place the taros on the oven rack and bake for 45 minutes. Add the potatoes to the oven and bake until the potatoes and taros are soft, about 1 hour more. When cool enough to handle, peel and put through the fine disk of a ricer or mash very well with a potato masher. Gently mix in the five-spice powder and nutmeg and a generous amount of salt, using your hands to combine the mixture very well and break up any lumps.

Make a well in the center of the mixture and place the yolks in it. Using your hands, work the egg yolks into the taro mixture around the edges of the well. Sprinkle ½ cup flour over the entire surface and lightly work the mixture together, adding more flour a little at a time if needed, until a dough forms.

Turn out the dough onto a lightly floured work surface and knead lightly just until smooth. Cut off a quarter of the dough, put the remainder aside, and cover with a kitchen towel. Roll the piece of dough into a rope about 1-inch thick. Using a sharp knife, slice the rope into 1-inch lengths. Roll each piece off a *gnocchi* paddle or dinner fork to make ridges all the way around (this helps the *gnocchi* to cook evenly). Repeat with the remaining dough.

Bring a large pot of salted water to a boil. Add half of the *gnocchi,* adjust the heat to a lively simmer, and simmer just until the *gnocchi* float to the top. As they rise, remove them with a slotted spoon to a sheet pan. Repeat with the remaining

gnocchi. (The recipe can be made in advance up to this point and kept refrigerated up to 1 day. Bring to room temperature before proceeding.)

Just before serving, melt 3 tablespoons butter in a large skillet over high heat. Add half the *gnocchi* and cook, shaking the pan occasionally, until heated through and browned, about 2 minutes. Transfer to a serving platter with a slotted spoon and keep warm. Wipe out the pan with a paper towel and repeat with the remaining butter and *gnocchi.* Serve immediately.

Lamb Smothered in Caramelized Onions and Spices with Parsley and Sweet Onion Salad

I think of this fragrant combination as my "onion lovers' dinner." I myself am the biggest onion lover I know, which is probably what inspired me to create a lamb stew that actually includes twice as much onion as lamb. The pleasure of this stew begins long before you taste it, as your house brims with the dizzying smell of onions cooked long and slow to bring out their sweetness. Caramelizing onions is the first step in countless Indian recipes; eventually the onions become so soft that they simply melt away, leaving their essence behind as the flavor base for the dish. Cooking the onions will take at least half an hour; don't try to rush it.

5 tablespoons canola oil

2 pounds lamb stew meat, preferably from the shoulder, cut into 1-inch pieces

8 large onions, thinly sliced

4 cloves garlic, minced

6 cloves

4 cardamom pods, crushed

½ to 1 teaspoon cayenne pepper

2 tablespoons garam masala (page 4)

1 cup lightly salted Chicken Stock (page 13), canned broth, or water

2 teaspoons tomato paste

2 medium-size tomatoes, quartered

1 cup thick yogurt (page 9; optional)

Basic Rice (page 10)

Parsley and Sweet Onion Salad (recipe follows)

Heat the oil over high heat in a large, heavy casserole or Dutch oven. Working in batches if needed to avoid crowding the pan, brown the meat all over, removing the pieces from the pan as they brown.

When all the meat is browned, pour off most of the fat that remains in the pan. Return the hot pan to the stove and add the onions. Cook, stirring often, until the onions are well caramelized, meltingly soft, and dark golden brown; this may take up to 30 minutes. Adjust the heat to prevent scorching, but keep it as high as possible. When the onions are about 5 minutes away from being fully cooked, add the garlic to the pan.

Return the browned lamb to the pot and add the cloves, cardamom, cayenne, and garam masala. Cook, stirring occasionally, until the spices turn dark brown and fragrant, 8 to 10 minutes. Add the stock, tomato paste, and tomatoes. Bring to a simmer, lower the heat, cover tightly, and cook at a bare simmer for 2 hours.

(The recipe can be made in advance up to this point, cooled to room temperature, and kept refrigerated up to 3 days.)

Before serving, bring the stew to a boil. If necessary, simmer uncovered until the liquid is reduced to a thick sauce. Turn off the heat and fold in the yogurt. Serve over rice with parsley and sweet onion salad.

Parsley and Sweet Onion Salad

MAKES
4 TO 6
SERVINGS

To play off the long-cooked, caramelized onions in this lamb dish, I like to serve a salad that includes pungent, refreshingly crisp raw onions. Sweet, fresh parsley sets off the onions perfectly. Flat-leaf Italian parsley has the best flavor. If you haven't ever thought of parsley as a salad green, let this recipe change your mind. If you can't find sweet onions, use regular onions, thinly sliced and soaked in several changes of cold water for about an hour.

3 cups Italian (flat-leaf) parsley, leaves only

1 large Vidalia, Walla Walla, or other sweet, mild onion (see note above), very thinly sliced

Freshly squeezed juice of 1 to 2 limes
Kosher salt

Just before serving, toss the parsley and onion together. Squeeze in the juice of 1 lime, sprinkle with salt, and toss. If the salad seems dry, squeeze in the other lime and toss again. Taste for salt and serve.

ROAST BONELESS LEG OF LAMB WITH SPICY CUMIN CRUST

I admit that this recipe contains a truly outrageous amount of cumin, not to mention black pepper. You can use less if you like (even half the amount), but trust me: To create the perfect spicy, earthy, crunchy crust for a meaty leg of lamb, the extreme measures are entirely worth it. To hold the crust together I use a moist puree of chipotle chiles in adobo, smoked jalapeños softened in a vinegary sauce. This is an easy and impressive entrée that produces the most fabulous leftovers in my kitchen: slices of tender, spiced lamb perfect for sandwiches, wraps, or the samosas on page 53. Be sure to cook the meat to medium-rare; each slice should be pink (not red or brown) in the center.

½ cup cumin seeds, toasted (page 12)
½ cup black peppercorns, toasted (page 12)
½ (2-ounce) can chipotle chiles in adobo, pureed until smooth
¼ to ½ cup canola oil

1 (6- to 8-pound) boneless leg of lamb, rolled and tied (your butcher can do this)
Kosher salt
Curried Lentil Puree (page 23; optional)
Cilantro sprigs, for garnish

Heat the oven to 400 degrees. In a spice grinder or coffee grinder, grind the cumin and peppercorns together (work in batches if necessary). Transfer to a small bowl and stir in the chipotle puree and ¼ cup oil.

Sprinkle the lamb all over with salt, then rub with the spice puree, adding the remaining oil to the puree if you are running low. Set on a rack in a roasting pan and roast for 30 minutes. Raise the heat to 450 degrees and roast 15 to 30 minutes more, or until medium-rare, my preference for lamb (rare lamb is chewy; well-done lamb is dry and flavorless). I test for doneness by slipping a sharp, thin knife into the roast and leaving it there for 30 seconds. Then I pull it out and press it against my lips; a warm but not intolerably hot blade means medium-rare meat.

Remove from the oven and let rest for 10 minutes. Slice and serve with curried lentil puree and garnish with cilantro.

LAMB WITH SPICED *KORMA* SAUCE AND *CHAPPATIS*

MAKES
4 TO 6
SERVINGS

I was first introduced to Indian cooking in my home city of Kuala Lumpur, Malaysia, which has a large Indian community, and since I was a child, I've loved the saucy, fragrant Indian dishes known as kormas. Meat, poultry, or vegetables are simmered in a spiced sauce of yogurt and ground nuts, creating a fantastic combination of tart, rich, and spicy flavors. The yogurt also tenderizes whatever you're cooking, so this is a great place to use meaty lamb shanks or venison stew.

I've converted the classic recipe into an easy one-pot dish that can be ready in under an hour. For a complete dinner you need nothing more than rice and a big green salad (I like to add sprigs of fresh cilantro when making a salad to serve with Indian food). To dress it up, make your own warm, fragrant chappatis (whole wheat flatbread) for soaking up the perfumed sauce.

½ cup coarsely chopped fresh ginger
3 cloves garlic
2 large onions, chopped
4 tablespoons clarified butter
   (page 2) or canola oil
2 tablespoons cardamom seeds
1 (3-inch) stick cinnamon
1 bay leaf
2 pounds lamb stew meat, preferably
   from the shoulder or the leg, cut into
   1-inch pieces
½ teaspoon turmeric
1 teaspoon cayenne pepper

1 teaspoon Aleppo chili pepper
   (page 1)
½ cup diced fresh or drained canned
   tomatoes
1 cup thick yogurt (page 9)
1 cup lightly salted Chicken Stock
   (page 13) or canned broth or water
½ cup cashew nuts, pulsed in a food
   processor just until ground
Cilantro leaves, for garnish
Whole-Wheat *Chappati* Breads
   (page 30) *or* Basic Rice (page 10),
   for serving

In a food processor, pulse the ginger, garlic, and onions together. In a large, heavy pot, heat the butter over medium-high heat. Add the cardamom, cinnamon, and bay leaf, and adjust the heat so that the spices do not burn. Cook, stirring, just until darkened and fragrant, about 30 seconds. Add the ginger mixture and cook, stirring, until the moisture evaporates and the vegetables start to soften and brown, about 10 minutes.

Season the lamb all over with turmeric, cayenne, and Aleppo pepper, and add to the pot. Raise the heat so that the meat is sizzling and cook, stirring occasionally, until the lamb is lightly browned all over. Stir in the tomatoes and yogurt, adjust the heat to a bare simmer (if the mixture is too hot at this point the yogurt may separate), and simmer 20 minutes, or until the liquid has reduced by about a third. Stir occasionally to make sure the bottom does not burn. Add the stock and simmer 10 minutes more. Just before serving, stir in the nuts and garnish with cilantro. Serve with *chappatis* or rice.

MALAYSIAN *SATAY* PARTY
WITH SESAME-CUCUMBER SALAD

MAKES 8
SERVINGS
(IF YOU
MAKE ALL
THE *SATAYS*)

When I was growing up in Malaysia, there was nothing I looked forward to more than our family satay parties. We all adored satays (they are popular all over Malaysia and Thailand) and made them out of meat, chicken, shellfish—even fruits like mango and pineapple. For the parties we each had our own individual hibachi to grill on.

The key to successful satays is to weave the meat onto the skewer so that the skewer itself is mostly covered. They cook quickly and should be passed out and eaten as they are cooked. I've given three of my favorite variations here, of which only the beef is truly a traditional satay. But they are all equally wonderful with the very traditional peanut sauce, spiked with tangy tamarind.

You'll need plenty of thin bamboo skewers about 8 inches long. Soak them for an hour or so beforehand to prevent burning.

BEEF *SATAY* WITH SPICY TURMERIC
AND LEMONGRASS MARINADE

1 tablespoon ground turmeric (freshly grated is even more delicious if you can find it)

¼ cup thinly sliced lemongrass, tough ends removed

¼ cup minced ginger

2 jalapeño chiles, stems removed

2 cloves garlic

2 pounds beef (tips of filet mignon are best, but any steak will work), cut into ¼-inch-thick slices (about 1-inch wide and as long as possible)

¼ cup soy sauce

¼ cup sugar

2 tablespoons *sambal* (page 8)

½ cup canola oil

In a mortar and pestle or a small food processor, pound or puree the turmeric, lemongrass, ginger, jalapeños, and garlic together into a paste. Add the beef and the remaining ingredients and marinate at least 2 hours or up to 8 hours before cooking.

To make the *satays*, push the skewer down the center of the strip of beef. The goal is to have as little of the skewer exposed to heat as possible, so try to keep the skewer *inside* the piece of meat. Exposed parts of the skewer can be covered by bunching up the meat. The result should be almost flat, and the meat should cover about two-thirds of the skewer. See page 204 about finishing the dish.

Lamb Satay with Garam Masala

2 tablespoons garam masala (page 4)
¼ cup minced fresh ginger
2 cloves garlic
½ cup loosely packed fresh mint leaves

2 pounds lamb loin or tenderloin,
    cut into ¼-inch-thick slices
    (about 1-inch wide and as long as
    possible)

In a mortar and pestle or a small food processor, pound or puree the garam masala, ginger, garlic, and mint together into a paste. Rub onto the lamb strips and let marinate at least 2 hours or up to 8 hours before cooking. Thread onto skewers as described above. See page 204 about finishing the dish.

CHICKEN *SATAY* WITH MARJORAM AND GARLIC MARINADE

1 cup loosely packed fresh marjoram or oregano leaves
5 cloves garlic
Freshly grated zest of 2 lemons
½ cup canola oil

4 chicken breast halves, pounded thin and cut into strips 1-inch wide
Kosher salt and freshly ground black pepper
Freshly squeezed juice of 2 lemons

Chop the marjoram and garlic together until fine. Transfer to a bowl and add the lemon zest and oil. Add chicken and marinate at least 30 minutes or up to 3 hours before cooking. Thread onto skewers as described above. Just before cooking, sprinkle the chicken with salt, pepper, and lemon juice. See below about finishing the dish.

TO FINISH THE DISH:
Spicy Peanut Sauce (recipe follows)
Sesame-Cucumber Salad (recipe follows)

Basic Rice (page 10)

To cook the *satays*, heat a grill to very hot. Grill the skewers just until browned on both sides and serve with spicy peanut sauce for dipping. Accompany with sesame-cucumber salad and rice if desired.

SPICY PEANUT SAUCE

MAKES
ABOUT
2 CUPS

2 tablespoons canola oil
4 large shallots, minced
1 large clove garlic, minced
2 teaspoons peanut oil
1 cup smooth peanut butter
½ cup ketchup
¼ to ½ cup tamarind paste (page 9)
¼ cup sugar

1 cup water or white wine
1 cup roasted peanuts, coarsely chopped
About 1 teaspoon apple cider vinegar
Sambal (page 8)
Kosher salt and freshly ground black pepper

Heat the canola oil in a deep skillet over high heat. Add the shallots and garlic, and cook, stirring often, until very soft. Adjust the heat to prevent scorching.

Add the peanut oil, peanut butter, ketchup, tamarind paste, sugar, and water, and stir until smooth. Bring to a simmer and simmer gently for 15 minutes, adding more liquid as needed if the mixture seems too thick.

Fold in the peanuts. Add 1/2 teaspoon vinegar, *sambal*, and salt and pepper to taste. Add more vinegar a little at a time until the sauce is rich and tangy.

SESAME-CUCUMBER SALAD

A simple but refreshing combination. The toasty sesame and cool cucumber go together perfectly.

MAKES
4 SERVINGS

2 cucumbers, peeled, seeded, and thickly
    sliced into half-moons
1/4 cup white sesame seeds, toasted
    (page 12) and coarsely ground
    in a mortar and pestle

Kosher salt and freshly ground black
    pepper

Put the cucumbers in a bowl. Just before serving, toss with the sesame seeds and salt and pepper to taste.

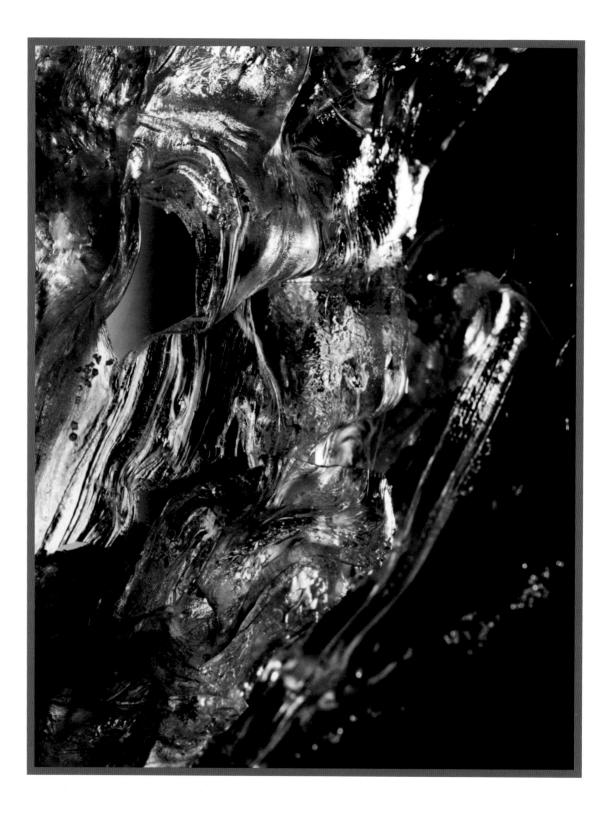

Desserts

COCONUT PARFAIT WITH MACADAMIA
BRITTLE, RUM CREAM, AND CHOCOLATE
SAUCE

SORBETS FROM AZ

STRAWBERRY-VANILLA

MANGO-LIME

MELON-MINT

LEMON-GINGER

INDIAN PISTACHIO ICE MILK *(KULFI)*

COOL FRUIT SOUP WITH TAMARIND SORBET

BLACK RICE PUDDING WITH MANGO

COCONUT AND PINEAPPLE FLAN WITH PALM
SUGAR SYRUP

DOUBLE-LIME AND GINGER CRÈME BRÛLÉE

EASY COCONUT CRÈME CARAMEL

CHOCOLATE-ORANGE POTS-DE-CRÈME

CANDIED GINGER SHORTBREAD

BANANA-NUT SPRINGROLL WITH CHOCOLATE
ICE CREAM

PUMPKIN BREAD PUDDING WITH PERSIMMON
FREEZE

STRAWBERRY-RHUBARB TART

COCONUT PARFAIT WITH MACADAMIA BRITTLE, RUM CREAM, AND CHOCOLATE SAUCE

This is really four recipes in one. Each component—the luscious coconut ice cream, the crunchy, caramelized shards of macadamia brittle, the pillowy rum-scented whipped cream, and the dark, dark chocolate sauce—has many uses in my dessert kitchen. All piled together, they are simply extraordinary. Or you might serve just the ice cream and the sauce. Or just the ice cream showered with brittle. Or the brittle with the sauce for dipping—you see, I could go on and on. I love them all and know you will, too.

The brittle goes especially well with some of the creamy desserts in this chapter, such as Double-Lime and Ginger Crème Brûlée (page 221) and Black Rice Pudding with Mango (page 218).

FOR THE ICE CREAM:
1 cup half-and-half
½ cup dry unsweetened coconut
2 cups coconut milk
1 vanilla bean, split lengthwise
7 egg yolks
¼ cup sugar

TO FINISH:
Macadamia Brittle (recipe follows)
Rum Cream (recipe follows)
Chocolate Sauce (recipe follows)

Make the ice cream: Combine the half-and-half and coconut in a saucepan. Bring to a simmer and let simmer for 15 minutes, then turn off the heat and set aside to infuse for at least 30 minutes and up to 2 hours. Strain the mixture into a large saucepan and add the coconut milk. Using the tip of a small sharp knife, scrape out the black vanilla seeds. Add both the seeds and the pod to the saucepan. Bring the mixture to a boil over medium heat and boil about 5 minutes.

Meanwhile, whisk the egg yolks and sugar together in a large bowl until lemon yellow and thick. Pour half of the hot coconut mixture into the egg mixture and whisk to combine. Pour the egg-coconut mixture back into the hot liquid in the saucepan and cook over medium heat until thickened, stirring constantly with a wooden spoon. At 160 degrees, the mixture will give off a puff of steam. When the mixture reaches 180 degrees, it will be thickened and creamy, like eggnog. If you don't have a thermometer, test it by dipping a wooden spoon into the mixture. Run your finger down the back of the spoon. If the stripe remains clear, the mixture is ready; if the edges blur, the mixture is not quite thick enough yet. When it is ready, quickly remove it from the heat.

In the meantime, half-fill a large bowl with ice water. Strain the mixture into a smaller bowl to smooth it and remove the vanilla bean. Rest the smaller bowl in the ice water and let the mixture cool, stirring often, then freeze according to the directions of your ice cream maker.

To make the parfaits, roughly chop up the cooled brittle. In tall glasses or bowls, layer spoonfuls of ice cream, rum cream, chocolate sauce, and brittle. End with a dollop of rum cream and a sprinkling of brittle bits.

MACADAMIA BRITTLE

1 cup macadamia nuts, toasted
   (page 11)
1 cup sugar

1 teaspoon salt
1 teaspoon baking powder

MAKES
ABOUT
8 SERVINGS

Butter a sheet pan and set aside.

Roughly chop the macadamia nuts. Heat the sugar in a heavy saucepan over medium heat. When the sugar starts to melt, turn the heat to low and stir constantly until the sugar melts and turns golden brown. Stir in the nuts, salt, and baking powder. Put the mixture on a sheet pan and spread out with a spatula to a 1/4-inch thickness (it will not fill the pan). Set aside to cool until hard. Break into pieces with your hands and store in an airtight container until ready to use.

Rum Cream

½ cup heavy cream

2 tablespoons sugar

2 tablespoons dark rum

Whip all the ingredients together until soft peaks form.

Chocolate Sauce

1 cup sugar

1 cup water

2 tablespoons pure vanilla extract

½ cup unsweetened cocoa powder

½ cup heavy cream

Combine the water and sugar in a small, heavy saucepan. Bring to a boil over high heat, stirring until the sugar dissolves. Remove from the heat and whisk in the vanilla, cocoa, and cream. Return to medium heat and cook, stirring often, until the sauce thickens. Let cool to room temperature.

Sorbets from AZ

Sweet, tart fruit sorbets make perfect desserts after the complex, lavishly spiced dishes I like to serve at Restaurant AZ. I usually combine one fruit and one flavoring, perhaps a freshening herb like mint, a fragrant aromatic like ginger, or a liqueur such as dark, spicy rum. Adding that little bit of liqueur also makes the sorbets easier to puree because the mixture will not freeze quite as hard when alcohol is present. You can make all of these sorbets with or without an ice cream maker.

EACH RECIPE
MAKES
ABOUT
6 SERVINGS

Strawberry-Vanilla

I pound ripe strawberries, hulled and
   quartered, or whole raspberries
½ cup ruby port

I cup sugar
I vanilla bean, split lengthwise
Freshly squeezed juice of I lemon

Combine all the ingredients in a nonreactive bowl and set aside to macerate for I hour. Remove the vanilla bean, transfer the mixture to a blender or food processor, and pulse just until pureed. Don't overprocess or the mixture will become thin and watery. Taste for sugar, adding more if needed (the mixture should taste just a little bit too sweet at room temperature; it will taste great when frozen).

If using an ice cream maker, proceed according to the manufacturer's instructions. If not, pour the mixture into ice cube trays and freeze.

Working in batches, pulse the ice cubes in a powerful blender or food processor to make a slushy "granita." Transfer to a bowl and keep frozen until ready to serve; you may need to let it soften at room temperature before serving.

Mango-Lime

Flesh of 2 very ripe mangoes
⅓ cup dark or light rum

Freshly squeezed juice and zest of 2 limes
½ cup sugar

Combine the ingredients in a blender or food processor and puree until smooth. Taste for sugar, adding more as needed (the mixture should taste just a little bit too sweet at room temperature; it will taste great when frozen). Freeze according to the instructions above.

Melon-Mint

2½ cups ripe melon chunks, such as
  Cavaillon, cantaloupe, or honeydew
¼ cup melon liqueur, such as Midori
  (optional)

2 tablespoons finely chopped mint
Freshly squeezed juice of 1 lime
½ cup sugar

Combine the ingredients in a blender or food processor and puree until smooth. Taste for sugar, adding more as needed (the mixture should taste just a little bit too sweet at room temperature). Freeze according to the instructions above.

Lemon-Ginger

4 lemons, scrubbed clean
1 cup chopped fresh ginger
  (no need to peel it)

2 cups water
1 cup honey

Cut the lemons in half and squeeze the juice into a saucepan, discarding any pits. Add the squeezed-out lemon halves to the saucepan, along with the ginger and water. Bring to a boil. Boil for 2 minutes, then turn off the heat and set aside to infuse for 30 minutes. Stir in the honey. Taste for sweetness, adding more honey as needed (the mixture should taste just a little bit too sweet at room temperature). Strain and let cool. Freeze according to the instructions above.

Indian Pistachio Ice Milk (Kulfi)

The perfect follow-up to richly spiced Indian curries is cool, soothing kulfi, *ice cream made from milk and nuts. The beauty of* kulfi *is that it's simply simmered and then frozen in molds, not churned in a machine like ice cream, so it's easy for anyone to make at home. I use evaporated milk for a little extra creaminess, but* kulfi *is meant to be cold and refreshing, not too rich. In India, the pistachio-green* kulfi *served on special occasions is decorated with gleaming shavings of edible gold.*

⅓ cup sugar
3 green cardamom pods
1 ¾ cups evaporated milk
¾ cup heavy cream
¾ cup toasted pistachio nuts
   (page 11), chopped

Diced fruit and/or chopped nuts, for
   garnish (such as mango, pineapple,
   macadamias, or pistachios)

Combine the sugar, cardamom, evaporated milk, and cream in a heavy saucepan. Heat to a simmer and simmer for 15 minutes. Remove the cardamom pods. Stir in the nuts, then turn off the heat and set aside to cool. Pour into molds or mugs, then freeze until solid, at least 8 hours. *(The recipe can be made in advance up to this point and kept refrigerated up to 2 days.)*

Serve garnished with diced fruit and/or chopped nuts.

Cool Fruit Soup
with Tamarind Sorbet

This fruit soup is easy, refreshing, and light, like a fruit salad but even more soothing. The sorbet adds a wonderfully tangy spark to the flavors; tamarind is often used in desserts and drinks in India, to cool off after a hot meal. But you can serve a different sorbet of your choice.

Crisp cookies, tuiles, or nut brittles are delicious with this smooth dessert.

FOR THE SORBET:
1 ½ cups sugar
2 ½ cups water
1 pound tamarind pulp (page 9)
2 cups orange juice
1 ½ cups club soda

FOR THE SOUP:
1 pineapple, peeled, cored, and coarsely chopped
2 mangoes, peeled, pitted, and coarsely chopped
Lime juice

Up to 2 days before serving, combine the sugar and 1 ½ cups water in a heavy pot and heat over medium heat, stirring until the sugar dissolves completely. Set aside.

Combine the tamarind pulp and the remaining 1 cup water in a medium pot and heat over medium heat. Whisk the mixture as it heats to break up lumps. As the water evaporates, gradually add the orange juice. Once all the juice has been added, simmer gently another 10 minutes. The mixture should have a thick, smooth consistency. Strain the tamarind to smooth it and to remove any seeds.

Whisk the tamarind pulp with ½ cup of the sugar syrup (reserve the rest for the fruit soup) and the club soda. Taste for sweetness, adding more syrup as needed (the mixture should taste just a little bit too sweet at room temperature; it will taste perfect when frozen). Freeze in an ice cream machine according to the manufacturer's instructions.

Make the soup: Puree the fruits in a food processor or blender. Add the remaining 1 cup of sugar syrup. Strain through a fine strainer and refrigerate until serving.

(The soup can be made in advance up to this point and kept refrigerated up to 1 day.)

Just before serving, season the soup to taste with lime juice, keeping in mind that the sorbet is quite tart. To serve, pour the chilled soup into bowls. Float 1 or 2 scoops of sorbet in each bowl.

BLACK RICE PUDDING WITH MANGO

MAKES
6 SERVINGS

This classic Thai dessert is very traditional and very easy. Although black rice sounds terribly exotic, it's simply sticky rice that hasn't had the bran removed (like any brown rice). The bran gives it a wonderful texture, perfect for rice pudding. Italian Arborio rice would work, too. The nutty rice needs nothing more than the creamy flavor of coconut to set it off, plus some juicy ripe mango on top for serving.

The custard also makes a perfect base for ice cream. Simply cool the mixture after cooking and turn it in an ice-cream maker until frozen and thick.

1 cup black or plain Sticky Rice (page 10), rinsed under running water until the water runs completely clear
3 cups water
4 cups coconut milk

¾ cup palm sugar (page 8) or brown sugar
½ teaspoon salt
2 large mangoes, peeled and diced, for serving

Combine the rice and water in a heavy saucepan and bring to a boil over high heat. Boil for 5 minutes, stirring often. Turn the heat to very low, cover, and simmer without stirring for 15 minutes. Stir in the coconut milk, sugar, and salt, and bring to a simmer, uncovered. Simmer, stirring often, until the coconut milk is very thick and the rice is very soft. The texture should be like hot cereal, quite soupy (it will thicken as it cools). Serve warm or chill in individual bowls. (*The recipe can be made in advance and kept refrigerated up to 2 days.*) Top each serving with diced mango.

COCONUT AND PINEAPPLE FLAN WITH PALM SUGAR SYRUP

When I was a child, my aunts often used to make this caramel custard dessert. If you like the flavor combination of a piña colada, imagine it as a cool dessert with an edge of burnt sugar from the caramel, and you'll know just how good this is.

My aunts would cook the custard on the stovetop, patiently waiting (with long skewers in hand) for bubbles to form so that they could pop each one, ensuring a perfectly smooth dessert. I'm afraid I don't have that kind of time! I bake the custard in a water bath for very smooth and creamy results. Bits of ripe pineapple add juicy texture.

FOR THE SYRUP:
½ cup palm sugar (page 8) or
    dark brown sugar
½ cup water

FOR THE CUSTARD:
5 eggs
½ cup sugar
1 cup coconut cream (page 2)
1 teaspoon pure vanilla extract
½ cup diced fresh pineapple, plus thin
    pineapple slices for garnish

Make the syrup: Combine the sugar and water in a heavy saucepan over low heat and simmer until reduced to a light syrup. Set aside to cool.

Prepare a water bath: Line a 2-inch-deep (at least) roasting pan with paper towels or newspapers. Arrange 4 to 6 ramekins, small bowls, or teacups in the pan, leaving room between them and making sure they are not touching the sides of the pan.

Make the custard: Beat the eggs, sugar, coconut cream, and vanilla together. Stir in the diced pineapple. Set aside for 30 minutes to let the mixture settle (this will prevent air bubbles in the finished dessert).

Heat the oven to 300 degrees. Divide the mixture among the ramekins. Fill the roasting pan with very hot water until it comes halfway up the sides of the ramekins.

Lightly cover the pan with a sheet of parchment paper or aluminum foil. Bake in the center of the oven for 25 minutes, or until a knife inserted in the center comes out clean. Remove from the water bath, tightly cover each ramekin with plastic wrap, and chill until ready to serve. *(The recipe can be made in advance up to this point and kept refrigerated up to 2 days.)*

Drizzle each serving with palm sugar syrup and serve, garnished with pineapple slices.

Double-Lime and Ginger Crème Brûlée

MAKES
8 SERVINGS

Lime juice and *lime zest, fresh ginger* and *candied ginger—I always enjoy using differ-ent versions of the same flavor, and lime and ginger are two of my favorites. Both of them travel smoothly between the savory and sweet parts of the meal, and they are fabulous together. The chopped candied ginger adds lovely chewy bits to the crème brûlée and is said to be very soothing to the stomach. To add yet another layer of ginger zip, serve the creamy custard with crisp Candied Ginger Shortbread (page 225).*

If you like, you can cook the custard on top of the stove in a double boiler instead of in the oven. It will take 15 to 20 minutes of frequent stirring to thicken. Add the candied ginger at the very end.

2½ cups heavy cream
1 vanilla bean, split lengthwise, insides
    scraped out with the tip of a sharp
    knife
7 egg yolks
3 tablespoons granulated sugar
1½ tablespoons freshly squeezed lime
    juice

Freshly grated zest of 2 limes
2 tablespoons finely minced fresh ginger
2 tablespoons minced candied ginger
3 tablespoons light brown sugar, sifted to
    remove any lumps, or coarse sugar

Up to 1 day before serving, cook the custard:

Prepare a water bath: Line a 2-inch-deep (at least) roasting pan with paper towels or newspapers. Arrange 8 ramekins or other cups in the pan, leaving room between them and making sure they are not touching the sides of the pan.

Heat the oven to 300 degrees.

Combine the cream, vanilla bean, and vanilla scrapings in a heavy saucepan. Heat over low heat until lukewarm to the touch. Remove the vanilla bean, leaving the scrapings in the cream (the bean can be rinsed, dried, and reused).

Whisk the egg yolks, granulated sugar, lime juice, zest, and fresh ginger together in a bowl. Slowly whisk in the warm cream. Whisk together, then stir in the candied ginger. Divide the mixture among the ramekins, filling them almost full. Fill the roasting pan with very hot water until it comes halfway up the sides of the ramekins.

Cover the entire pan with aluminum foil. Bake in the center of the oven until almost set but still a bit soft in the center, 30 to 40 minutes. The custard should "shimmy" a bit when you shake the pan; it will firm up more as it cools.

Remove from the water bath and let cool 15 minutes. Tightly cover each ramekin with plastic wrap, making sure the plastic does not touch the surface of the custard. Refrigerate until cold, at least 2½ hours. (The recipe can be made in advance up to this point and kept refrigerated up to 2 days.)

When ready to serve, heat a broiler to very hot (or fire up your kitchen blow torch). Uncover the chilled custards. Coat the top of each custard completely with an even layer of brown sugar.

Place the ramekins on a baking sheet or in a roasting pan and broil until the sugar is melted and well browned, 1 to 2 minutes. Let cool 1 minute before serving.

Easy Coconut Crème Caramel

My dinner dishes are often intense in flavor and crisp in texture, so dessert is when I am ready to surrender to a creamy, soothing custard. This recipe is much simpler and more forgiving than most crème caramels (which are full of egg yolks and tend to get gluey), with egg whites for lightening and condensed milk for rich flavor. Coconut milk is a wonderful ingredient for desserts; it's so sweet, luscious, and creamy on its own that you hardly have to do anything to it!

FOR THE CARAMEL:
1 cup sugar
½ cup unsweetened coconut flakes

FOR THE CUSTARD:
10 eggs
4 cups (1 quart) milk
1 cup coconut milk
1 cup condensed milk

Make the caramel: Melt the sugar in a heavy pot over high heat, stirring constantly and carefully until the sugar melts into a golden brown caramel. Remove from the heat and stir in the coconut. Pour the caramel into an 8-inch cake pan or divide it among 8 small (2-ounce) ramekins or tartlet pans. Let cool.

Make the custard: Mix all the ingredients together until well blended. Pour over the cooled caramel.

Preheat the oven to 375 degrees. Prepare a water bath: Line a roasting pan with paper towels or newspapers (this will keep the baking dishes from sliding around). Arrange the baking dish or dishes in the roasting pan, leaving room between them and making sure they are not touching the sides of the pan. Fill the pan with very hot water until it comes halfway up the sides of the dishes. Bake for 40 minutes (15 minutes for individual custards). The custard should still be wobbly in the center. Set aside to cool at room temperature.

To unmold, run a knife around the edge of the dish (or dishes). Dip the bottom of the dish in hot water to loosen the caramel. Turn out on a serving platter.

Chocolate-Orange Pots-de-Crème

MAKES
4 TO 6
SERVINGS

Chocolate and orange is an irresistible variation on the theme of sweet-and-citrus. A breath of orange scents the chocolate and the cream, giving the whole dessert an appealing lightness. In England, which is true heaven for chocolate lovers, you can buy whole balls of orange-flavored chocolate already shaped into wedges. This pudding is the next best thing and so easy that a child can make it. I know because I often made it as a child myself.

¾ cup heavy cream
½ cup whole milk
4 egg yolks
⅜ cup sugar

5 ounces unsweetened chocolate, chopped
1 tablespoon pure orange extract

Prepare a water bath: Line a 2-inch-deep (at least) roasting pan with paper towels or newspapers. Arrange 4 to 6 ramekins, small bowls, or teacups in the pan, leaving room between them and making sure they are not touching the sides of the pan.

Heat the oven to 375 degrees. Combine the cream and milk in a heavy saucepan and bring to a boil. Meanwhile, whisk the egg yolks and sugar together until pale and smooth. Pour the hot cream over the egg mixture and stir. Add the chocolate and orange extract, and stir until the chocolate melts. If desired, strain to remove any lumps.

Divide the mixture among the ramekins. Fill the roasting pan with very hot water until it comes halfway up the sides of the ramekins. Bake in the center of the oven for 30 minutes, or until the custard is just set in the center. Remove from the water bath and chill until ready to serve, at least 2½ hours. *(The recipe can be made in advance and kept refrigerated up to 2 days.)* Serve cold.

Candied Ginger Shortbread

MAKES

4 TO 6

SERVINGS

Alongside cool sorbets, creamy custards, and lush ice creams, I like to serve some-thing crisp and light. When I lived in England as a young girl, I fell in love with short-bread, especially the popular kind that was scented with familiar candied ginger. It works beautifully with Asian-inspired meals. The cookies are also wonderful with fra-grant teas like Darjeeling or milky chai.

When you roll the dough into a circle and cut it into wedges like a pie, the cookie shape is known as a "petticoat tail." But you can also cut the dough into bars, circles, or any shape you like.

2¼ cups all-purpose flour
1 cup sugar, plus extra for dusting
1 teaspoon baking powder
1 pinch of salt
1 pound (4 sticks) cold unsalted butter,
   cut into pieces

1 teaspoon finely minced fresh ginger
2 tablespoons cold water
2 teaspoons minced candied ginger

Heat the oven to 350 degrees.

Thoroughly combine the flour, sugar, baking powder, and salt in a large bowl. Using your fingers, rub the butter and ginger into the mixture until it has the tex-ture of coarse crumbs. Gently mix in the water, then gather into a ball. Wrap it in plastic wrap and refrigerate at least 10 minutes or up to 30 minutes.

Press the dough into a 10-inch tart pan (or roll it out on a lightly floured sur-face into a circle about ¼ inch thick, then transfer to a cookie sheet). Using the tip of a sharp knife or a pizza cutter, lightly score the dough, cutting lines across the circle again and again to make pie-shaped wedges. Sprinkle the surface with the candied ginger and dust with extra sugar. Bake about 20 minutes, until dry and crisp; the shortbread will not brown. As the shortbread comes out of the oven, cut through the lines again. Let cool, gently break into petticoat tails, and serve. *(The recipe can be stored in an airtight container up to 2 days.)*

Banana-Nut Springroll with Chocolate Ice Cream

Cooking foods that span many cultures, as I do, you quickly learn that some things are truly universal. From strudel to springrolls, everyone loves a soft, melting filling rolled in a crisp, flaky crust. To make this dessert, bananas and cashews are rolled with brown sugar and butter to make a fragrant filling for Mediterranean phyllo dough, then served with chocolate ice cream. The roll is baked whole, then sliced for serving, so it's easy to assemble but still crisp and melting at the end.

I add a starchy plantain to the filling because it helps the roll keep its shape, but you can substitute a banana.

FOR THE BANANA FILLING:
1/2 yellow plantain, peeled with a sharp
    knife and cut into 1/4-inch dice or
    1 small banana
2 tablespoons melted butter
1 1/2 large ripe bananas
2 teaspoons dark brown sugar
1/4 teaspoon salt
1 teaspoon pure vanilla extract

TO FINISH THE DISH:
5 sheets phyllo dough, thawed if frozen
    and kept moist under a damp towel
1/3 cup melted butter
1/3 cup chopped toasted cashews or other
    nuts (page 11)
1/4 cup sugar
Chocolate ice cream, for serving

Heat the oven to 350 degrees. Toss the plantain with the melted butter in a roasting pan and roast for 15 minutes (if not using plantain, skip this step). Let cool and mix in the ripe bananas, sugar, salt, and vanilla until the mixture is smooth.

Heat the oven to 375 degrees.

Lay a sheet of phyllo on a work surface. Brush it all over with melted butter, then sprinkle with about one-fifth of the nuts and sugar. Cover with another sheet of phyllo. Repeat with melted butter, nuts, and sugar. Repeat the process until all 5 sheets of phyllo are stacked and covered with butter, nuts, and sugar.

Spoon the banana along one long edge of the phyllo dough (this is where you'll start to roll). Fold in both ends to hold the filling in as you roll. Gently roll up the filling in the phyllo (don't worry if it cracks) and place on a baking sheet. Brush the roll all over with melted butter. Bake for 15 to 20 minutes, or until golden brown. Let cool at least 10 minutes before serving to let the filling firm up a bit.

To serve, slice the roll into 1-inch lengths. Serve with chocolate ice cream.

PUMPKIN BREAD PUDDING WITH PERSIMMON FREEZE

FALL / WINTER

Here's my Thanksgiving dessert favorite, packed with the seasonal flavors of spices, pumpkin, nuts, and persimmon. You can certainly serve the warm, fragrant pudding without the persimmon freeze or with scoops of vanilla ice cream in its place. But I love the tart, icy accent that the persimmon provides. Persimmons are native to Asia and America, and come into season in the fall. The Japanese Hachiya persimmons become very soft and sweet as they ripen.

Each step of this recipe can be done well in advance, including baking the pudding. Re-warm it in the oven just before serving, at about 250 degrees.

FOR THE PUMPKIN BREAD:
1 ¾ cups sifted all-purpose flour
¼ teaspoon baking powder
1 teaspoon baking soda
1 teaspoon salt
½ teaspoon ground cinnamon
¼ teaspoon ground cloves
1 ⅓ cups sugar
⅓ cup shortening
2 eggs
1 cup canned pumpkin puree (not
    seasoned pumpkin pie filling)
⅓ cup milk
½ cup chopped walnuts
⅓ cup raisins or currants

FOR THE PERSIMMON FREEZE:
6 ripe Hachiya persimmons
1 lime

FOR THE PUDDING:
10 eggs
1 cup milk
1 cup heavy cream
1 teaspoon each ground cinnamon,
    nutmeg, and ginger
1 cup sugar

Up to 3 days before making the pudding, make the pumpkin bread: Heat the oven to 350 degrees and butter a loaf pan.

Sift together the sifted flour, baking powder, baking soda, salt, cinnamon, and cloves. In a large bowl, cream the sugar, shortening, and eggs together until light, smooth, and fluffy. Mix in the pumpkin puree. Add one-third of the dry ingredients and one-third of the milk to the mixture and beat just until smooth. Repeat twice more with the remaining dry ingredients and milk. Gently stir in the nuts and raisins. Pour the batter into the prepared pan and bake about 1 hour, or until the top is dry and springy and a tester inserted in the cake comes out clean. Let cool.

Make the persimmon freeze: Scoop out the flesh of the persimmons into a bowl or food processor. Mash or puree until almost smooth, squeezing the juice of the lime into the persimmon flesh. Freeze until ready to serve. *(The whole recipe can be made up to 2 days in advance up to this point.)*

Make the pudding: Heat the oven to 375 degrees.

In a large, shallow bowl, whisk all the ingredients together. Slice the pumpkin bread about 1/2 inch thick and lay the slices in the pudding. Let soak about 30 minutes. Arrange the slices in a large baking dish or roasting pan and pour any remaining pudding over them. Bake the pudding for 45 minutes, then raise the heat to 400 degrees and bake another 10 to 15 minutes, until lightly browned on top and a tester inserted in the center comes out clean. Let sit at least 15 minutes before serving. Serve warm with a scoop of persimmon freeze on each serving.

STRAWBERRY-RHUBARB TART

Sweet berries and tart rhubarb are a natural combination for me. I always like a hint of sourness to set off flavors, like a squeeze of lemon juice in a cup of sweet tea. Some people believe that they don't like rhubarb, but I think that's because it's too often overcooked, making it (let's be frank) stringy and slimy. Here, the rhubarb isn't simmered but simply tossed with sugar and baked on top of the tart until the sugar caramelizes. The result is irresistibly crunchy-sweet, almost candied.

If you like, serve the tart with crème fraîche that is lightly whipped for stiffness.

FOR THE DOUGH:
12 tablespoons (1 ½ sticks) unsalted
   butter, softened to room temperature
½ cup packed light brown sugar
1 egg
1 ½ cups all-purpose flour
Pinch of salt

FOR THE FILLING:
2 cups strawberries, hulled and thickly
   sliced
8 ounces rhubarb, cut into ¼-inch lengths
¼ cup light brown sugar
2 tablespoons all-purpose flour

Make the dough: In a mixer, cream the butter until smooth. Add the sugar and cream together until smooth. Beat in the egg. Add the flour and salt, and mix just until blended. Flatten the dough into a thick disk, wrap in plastic wrap, and chill for at least 2 hours or overnight. (If chilled overnight, let sit at room temperature for 15 minutes before rolling out.)

Half an hour before removing the dough from the refrigerator, make the filling: Toss all the ingredients together. Set aside.

Heat the oven to 400 degrees.

On a lightly floured surface, roll out the dough into a large circle, 10 to 11 inches. Don't worry if the edges are rough; you'll be folding them over. Transfer the circle to a baking sheet. Spread the filling over the circle, spreading it to within 1 inch of the edge. Fold the edge up and over the filling, encasing it and making a thick edge for the tart. Bake for 15 minutes, then lower the heat to 350 degrees and bake until the crust is golden brown, 30 to 35 minutes more. Let cool at least 15 minutes before serving.

SOURCES

Most of the ingredients in this book can be found in a large supermarket or in any Asian market. If you are looking elsewhere, these are my own favorite suppliers.

FOR ALL KINDS OF ASIAN AND
SOUTHEAST ASIAN INGREDIENTS:

Asia Market
Phone: 212-962-2020 or 2028
Fax: 212-962-3391

FOR ALL KINDS OF SPICES, LENTILS,
DRIED FRUITS, AND OTHER INDIAN AND
MIDDLE EASTERN INGREDIENTS:

Kalustyan Importing Co.
Phone: 212-685-3451
Fax: 212-683-8458
Internet: www.kalustyans.com

Sahadi's Importing Co.
Phone: 718-624-4550
Fax: 718-643-4415
Internet: www.sahadis.com

FOR ALL KINDS OF JAPANESE PRODUCTS:

Katagiri Japanese Grocers
Phone: 212-755-3566
Fax: 212-752-4197
Internet: www.katagiri.com

FOR SMOKED FISH:

**Browne Trading Company of Portland,
   Maine**
Phone: 207-775-3118

INDEX